The Gosport Society

GOSPORT

CONSERVATION AND HERITAGE

T0333556

EDITED BY LOUIS MURRAY

The History Press

The Gosport Society

*A Gosport Society publication in association with
The History Press and within the framework of the
Heritage Action Zone (HAZ) Programme of Historic England.*

First published 2023

The History Press
97 St George's Place, Cheltenham,
Gloucestershire, GL50 3QB
www.thehistorypress.co.uk

British Library Cataloguing in Publication Data.
A catalogue record for this book is available from the British Library.

ISBN 978 0 7509 9930 4

Typesetting and origination by The History Press
Printed and bound in Great Britain by TJ Books Limited, Padstow, Cornwall.

Trees for Life

CONTENTS

ACKNOWLEDGEMENTS

PHOTO ATTRIBUTIONS

Initials accompanying each photographic image in the text attribute the image to its photographer or source. Where images were commissioned on a commercial basis, this is indicated below* and the company title and address are provided. Other images were provided at the discretion of the photographers and this is gratefully acknowledged here.

GP – *Goodwins Photography, 15 Northcross Street, Gosport, Hampshire, PO12 1BE.

LM – Louis Murray private collection.

GBC – Gosport Borough Council.

BP – *Browne Photographics, 5 Ariel Close, Lee-on-the-Solent, Hampshire, PO12 9FT.

HDS – Historical Diving Society.

RM – Richard Martin Gallery.

RW – Robert Whiteley.

GSA – Gosport Society image archive.

HM – Hovercraft Museum, Lee-on-the-Solent.

GRS – Gosport Railway Society.

PROJECT SUPPORT

The following agencies and individuals have supported this project in a variety of ways.

Grant moneys to assist in the production of the book have been gratefully received from Gosport Borough Council (GBC) and the Hampshire Archives Trust.

Robert Lihou Creative Services provided assistance with manuscript file handling and graphic representation.

Michelle Lees, the Heritage Action Zone (HAZ) manager at GBC, recorded progress on the work at HAZ Partnership quarterly meetings as part of Project 18. She also acted as liaison officer with Historic England in the concept developments phases of Project 18.

Brian Mansbridge, honorary treasurer of The Gosport Society, undertook bookkeeping and payment responsibilities in respect of the joint financing of the project by The Gosport Society, The History Press of Cheltenham, GBC and the Hampshire Archives Trust.

Staff at the Gosport Discovery Centre in Gosport, the Powder Monkey brewery and public house in Priddy's Hard and the Hovercraft Museum in Lee-on-the-Solent, who offered access to premises and directions. Members of the Friends of Gosport Museum, who provided access and commentary to parts of the collection of the Gosport Museum and SEARCH Gallery.

The national agency Historic England provided a framework for discussion of an 'informed conservation publication' in the initial phases of their Heritage Action Zone programme as it pertained to the award of HAZ status to Gosport and the emergence in 2019 of a partnership to carry the programme forward. The Gosport Society adopted special responsibility for Project 18 under this programme.

Thanks are due to many of the residents of Gosport, the primary audience for this book, professional officers at GBC, and the members of The Gosport Society who have taken an interest in the project from the start.

INTRODUCTION

This book is a product of the long involvement of The Gosport Society and GBC in the conservation and, in many cases, restoration and repurposing of the built estate in the ancient Borough of Gosport in Hampshire, bordering The Solent, the sheltered part of the English Channel that separates the Isle of Wight from the mainland.

The Gosport Society has joined The History Press to produce an illustrated compendium of articles on indicative and interesting features and achievements of the heritage, social history and conservation movements as they pertain in this geographically unique corner of south-east Hampshire. The book may be considered part of the wider set of expressions championed by the national agency Historic England under its HAZ Programme. Similarly, the articles that make up the chapters of this book – written from the standpoint of direct and personal experience of each author – contribute to the ongoing and fascinating 800-year-old story of a maritime town inescapably connected with the defence of the realm.

WHY IS THE BOOK NEEDED?

- It will be a legacy volume for the five-year (2019–23)Heritage Action Zones (HAZ) programme of Historic England. The prestigious HAZ status was accorded to Gosport in 2019.
- The compendium character of the volume – accounts by expert authors linking themes of civic history to the defence-of-the-realm built estate, to modern imperatives for urban regeneration – reflects a holistic and lasting perspective on the need to protect and enhance what, in UK-wide landscape asset terms is a unique heritage, for future generations to know and enjoy.
- A published and comprehensive, but always readable, telling of the story of Gosport is needed for ready use by municipal officers,

council-tax-paying residents, conservation architects and visitors drawn from far afield to the international tourist attractions of Gosport such as the Diving Museum at Stokes Bay, Explosion: The Museum of Naval Firepower at Priddy's Hard and the Royal Navy Submarine Museum at Haslar.

- Recently researched accounts of significant buildings, such as Bury House at Alverstoke and the ancient Church of St Mary the Virgin in Rowner, are given public acknowledgement in this book. The accounts contribute to architectural and archaeological knowledge. They have become part of the accumulated wisdom that is now part of the archival record, helping to broaden public recognition of the heritage assets register in Gosport.
- The book is expected to become a companion guide and backdrop to the successful and nationwide Heritage Open Days (HODs) festivals held throughout the nation annually in September. The Gosport Society was instrumental in helping to create HODs, probably the most widespread heritage and community history event in the country, more than twenty-five years ago.

Dr Louis Murray
The Gosport Society
Lee-on-the-Solent
May 2022

I

GOSPORT HERITAGE: CHALLENGES AND CHANGES OVER THE PAST TWENTY-FIVE YEARS – THE PERSPECTIVE OF A CONSERVATION PROFESSIONAL

Robert Harper

Gosport is a remarkable town. It is a place Historic England have described as being full of hidden gems. For such a small borough it has an exceptionally rich legacy of military sites. It is only in the last twenty-five years that we have begun to properly understand the true significance of the area as former military locations, fenced and wired off to the general public for decades, have come up for redevelopment. The challenge has been to ensure that the many historic buildings within these areas, and indeed across the borough, are given new life and secured in meaningful ways for future generations.

Gosport was fortunate in having resident and reputable local historian Lesley Burton as a strong champion of local heritage. This is brilliantly revealed in the numerous Gosport Society publications she was instrumental in publishing down the years. Beyond these, the breadth of published material on the social and civic history of the borough has been uneven. So, it has become crucial to gather and archive as much historic background information as possible through detailed research, input from expert consultants, archaeological surveys and local historians to ensure that the unique features of historic sites are properly recorded and understood so as to appropriately inform planning decisions and any subsequent repurposing and commercial development.

It is well worth giving an overview of just how multi-layered and complex Gosport history is by providing a brief summary of how the borough came to be what we see and know today.

There is early evidence of human activity in the Alver Valley and along the coast by hunter-gatherer communities. More settled evidence is shown in possible tumuli near Bury Cross and the partial remains of a suspected long barrow on Browndown North.

The Hampshire county archaeologist, David Hopkins, believes that the grid-like field systems covering the southern half of the borough, seen on old maps and reflected in much of the road layout today, may be evidence of potentially ancient field systems known as 'ladders'. If the area was intensely farmed, this may explain the lack of evidence for Roman settlement. It is, however, difficult to pin down what was happening in the post-Roman Dark Ages. At that time, the area was in the heart of territory controlled by the incomers who history refers to as Jutes.

The more evidenced and subsequent centuries of Saxon settlement can be seen in place names such as Alverstoke, Elson, Privett and Rowner. There is also archaeological evidence of a Saxon settlement north-east of Grange Farm, excavated as the Rowner redevelopment was under way in the post-Second World War period. Perhaps therefore, it is no surprise that the Normans chose a key crossing point over the Alver River, near the modern and popular Apple Dumpling Bridge. This was close to this settlement, as is the location of a postulated motte and bailey, now a scheduled ancient monument.

In the medieval period the area was still relatively lightly populated. The borough is fortunate in having several buildings still extant: the stone core of the Old Rectory in Alverstoke; St Mary the Virgin old church at Rowner; Le Breton Farmhouse and Court Barn in Lee-on-the-Solent; and some timber-framed, thatched cottages in Alverstoke and Rowner. While the field systems remained in the south and west, the northern part of the borough underwent gradual forest clearance through 'assarting', where small, irregular fields and farmsteads were carved out of woodland that may have once stretched to the Forest of Bere to the north.

The most indicative features of the landscape are, perhaps, in and around the Alver Valley. The southern section of Grange Farm retains parts of an original medieval Cistercian lay-brothers' farm. The Cistercians uniquely set up a system where the primary house (in this instance, Quarr Abbey on the Isle of Wight) developed a wide system of farms to exploit the countryside and bring in funds for the order. The Cistercians were leading experts on the use of water power and it can be no coincidence that their *grange* was established alongside the River Alver, nor that early maps show a highly complex system of water meadows extending for some distance. Recognisable parts of these still survive north and west of Grange Farm.

Gosport appeared as a new settlement in the early thirteenth century, close in time to the appearance of Portsmouth, across the harbour. Both were built to a rough grid of streets (in Gosport these are High Street, North Street, South Street and connecting north–south roads and alleys). Was the near-contemporary date a coincidence, or was this an attempt by the two sides of the harbour to compete for trade? With French raids beginning during the following century, it is clear that both sides of the harbour struggled to develop to their potential.

It is, in fact, the strategic importance of Gosport, and its vulnerability, that began to shape the landscape in the following centuries and why it became the focus for extensive military activity. First came a blockhouse at the harbour entrance to impede future raids, then under Henry VIII came earthworks nearby, and Haselworth Castle on or near the present-day Fort Monckton: all three clearly illustrated on a famous Cowdray engraving.

Leland described Gosport as a small fishing village. However, cartographic evidence suggests a more developed town with at least one substantial house in the vicinity of North Street and another large Jacobean building on the waterfront soon after 1600. The English Civil War had a direct impact, with the town used as the springboard for the bombardment, assault and capture of Portsmouth for Parliament, and a later Royalist revenge attack resulting in over twenty houses being burnt to the ground.

The Civil War was quickly followed by the Dutch Wars and, following the infamous raid on the Thames and Medway, a Dutch fleet sailed along the south coast threatening security. Three years later, Gosport prepared for future attacks by building earthworks around the town. In 1670, and known as the Gosport Lines, they included two small forts (Fort James on Borough Island and Fort Charles now under the former Camper & Nicholson boatyard site) and a substantial gun battery at Blockhouse. These early defences were designed to stop a landward bombardment of Portsmouth's developing dockyard and were extended or adapted with almost every future threat. New demi-bastions were added at Blockhouse at the beginning of the eighteenth century; a northern extension to the Gosport Lines around 1760, including closing access to Priddy's Hard; a panicked upgrade was instigated in the 1770s when news came of a Franco-Spanish 'armada' en route to the area in 1779; further upgrades proceeded in the Napoleonic Wars and a final overhaul of the Gosport Lines was undertaken around 1848 at a time of international tension.

The limited works of Henry VIII in Stokes Bay were replaced with several small artillery redoubts built to cover this potential invasion and landing point around 1781; Fort Monckton by 1790; outworks to Monckton and moats in the 1830s and two earth batteries on Browndown around 1852. These were soon followed by the Stokes Bay Lines: a long moat intersected with powerful gun batteries and an earth rampart for infantry. While these Lines were under construction, huge defensive forts were added at Blockhouse, Elson, Brockhurst, Rowner, Grange, Gomer and finally Gilkicker, closing landward access to the peninsula and securing additional firepower over Spithead. Gosport had effectively become one huge fortification.

Yet the defensive works did not stop there. As ordnance and warships developed, so new layers of defences appeared. Gosport has good examples of late nineteenth and early twentieth-century mass-concrete gun platforms, searchlight platforms, coastal defences from both world wars, and pill boxes along the Alver Valley, the coast north of Hardway, near Brockhurst and at Gilkicker.

In the Second World War, the significance of the town as a defensive hub was reflected in tank traps deployed just north of Fort Brockhurst and in the Alver Valley, while barrage balloon tethers within Fort Rowner are a reminder of the later threat by air. Indeed, Fort Blockhouse was the focus of the mining engineers in the late nineteenth century, specifically employed to oversee the deployment of minefields (both electrically operated and magnetic) on the harbour approaches, and the deployment of the first submarines at Fort Blockhouse, or HMS *Dolphin*, as the submarine home of the Royal Navy came to be called.

WIDER STRATEGIC SIGNIFICANCE

The fortifications described above highlight the complexity of the remarkable heritage of Gosport. But they reveal only a part of the civic story. As the fortifications appeared, and the naval base grew, so the strategic significance of the area was reflected in the growing involvement of all branches of the military:

- Private victualling on contract to the Royal Navy in the eighteenth century was subsumed by the Admiralty in the 1740s at Weevil, then expanded significantly in the 1760s and 1820s to become Royal Clarence Victualling Yard, one of three major naval supply depots in Britain.

- Haslar Royal Naval Hospital, claimed to be the biggest brick building in the world at the time of construction in 1746, was one Royal Navy answer to effectively imprisoning sick sailors behind high walls to prevent the loss of ships' crews through desertion.
- Numerous barracks complexes, for example, St George (1860s), Haslar (around 1802) and Browndown (the late 1800s), all remind us that troops were deployed here both to garrison the town and to move back and forth across the Empire and in time of war.

The Admiralty Experimental Works (now Qinetiq Marine Technology Park Haslar), set up by William Froude (1810–79), the 'father of hydrodynamics', is where naval ship design was thoroughly tested by scale models in the ship-testing tanks. The most fascinating discovery on this site in recent years was the Cavitation Tunnel. This is a huge, three-storey, hollow cylinder through which water could be pumped at varying speeds and from which propellers could be tested to minimise their sound signature and look for potential calibration problems. This example was constructed by Seimens-Schukert in the Second World War and was originally located in Hamburg. After the war, the entire tunnel and supporting machinery was brought back to this site and by the early 1950s was back in use within a purpose-built building, now Grade-II listed. A recent report by Historic England highlights the exceptional historic importance of this site.

The former Royal Naval Hospital Haslar. A major residential redevelopment project in Gosport some twenty years in the making. (GP)

The needs of the modern Royal Navy have meant that original structures of the oil fuel depot on Mumby Road could not realistically be retained. Research indicated that the site originated around 1907 with the first use of diesel-powered warships. The fuel was held in the many tanks on the site that, in many cases, dated from 1914. Machinery that operated all the pipes remained intact within a pump house at the north-west corner of the site and much of this dated from around 1907. In close liaison with the MoD archaeologist, the site was fully recorded, including the extent of the outworks to the ramparts along the eastern part of the site.

The Crimean War-era Gunboat Yard on Haslar Road is also unique to Gosport. It was clear during the conflict that the Russian Navy was reticent to come out of port to face allied fleets, so shallow-hulled gunboats were needed to move in close to bombard both ships and fortifications. The Gunboat Yard was constructed and used to house and repair a substantial fleet of such craft. While the site was reduced in capacity after that war, many of the original buildings and structures on site survive and have been written about at length by Historic England. It is perhaps from this site that Britain became notorious for its use of 'gunboat diplomacy' in the later nineteenth century.

AND STILL THE STORY CONTINUES

The former HMS *Daedalus* site in Lee-on-the-Solent (now known as Solent Airport) is one of the oldest and most unique military aviation sites in the UK. It lays claim to have been in at the birth of naval aviation around the time of the First World War and is noted especially for seaplane operations. Parts of the site were designated as a conservation area in 1999.

The Grange Airfield (around 1910), on the western edge of Gosport and fronting the Alver Valley, was eventually subsumed within HMS *Sultan*, the current Royal Navy aero- and marine-engineering training establishment. The modern base still retains many buildings relating to its earlier operational use for flight training and fighter squadrons. These are visible along Military Road. However, the original runways and aircraft taxiways have long been buried under housing estates.

The former submarine operational and training base at Fort Blockhouse retains a concentration of buildings and structures related to this former function. Therein lies the richest legacy of submariners' buildings in Britain, included in the 1990s as part of the Haslar Peninsula Conservation Area. Understanding of the site has greatly benefited from the knowledge shared by writer-researcher Chris Donnithorne. Several buildings have been listed on the site and the scheduled area of the fort has recently been extended.

The *c*.1802 workshops of the Royal Military Artificers, which were directly involved in developing and repairing the defences across the area, were identified in Royal Clarence Yard and listed in around 2000. Similarly, endeavours have been made to unravel the complicated archaeology across the site of the St Vincent sixth-form college on Mumby Road. These include the site of the mill on Forton Creek, to the back of the college, and foundations revealing the extent of the military hospital of around 1796. Later buildings associated with the basing of the Royal Marine Light Infantry here are a reminder that on many military sites there is more beneath the surface than is still visible.

Further research is needed to help the understanding of the role and function of RN Coastal Forces, who operated from Haslar Creek under the general command of HMS *Hornet* until after the Second World War. The site, encompassing the Joint Services Adventurous Sail Training Centre and adjacent to the Gunboat Yard, straddles both sides of Haslar Bridge and is within a conservation area.

Provisional and ongoing research points to a probable system of First World War practice trenches on Browndown North. The system seems indicated on an aerial photograph of the 1950s and closely replicates a sketch of trench systems from an officer's manual of 1917. We know the area was used for training in the First World War, but to have what appears to be two opposing sets of trenches across a no-man's-land is probably unique in Britain and now requires more intense research to put names and regiments to the site.

Several military graveyards (including what may be an extensive one beneath the Qinetiq Haslar Road site), isolation hospitals on the upper foreshore of Portsmouth Harbour, and extensive munitions and gunpowder depots complete with military narrow-gauge railway lines are part of the relict landscape of Gosport. Ditto, Forton Prison, with its history as a hospital and prisoner-of-war camp over an extended period before its remodelling as a military prison. Researcher Abigail Coppins has completed useful work on the significant number of black prisoners held there during the French Revolutionary Wars.

Evidence for sea salt farming can be seen in a good surviving example of a 'salting', off the coast near Fleetlands, clearly shown on early seventeenth-century maps. To this needs to be added the development of new settlements that are largely the result of inward military investment: Newtown, Camdentown and Angleseyville in the early to mid-nineteenth century and the military estates in Hardway, Rowner and Bedenham in the twentieth century.

While the military was long omnipresent in Gosport, local trades such as brewing and the building of both naval and civilian vessels also played an important part in shaping the town. Blakes' Brewery public houses, with their ornate, tiled fronts and now largely converted to homes, may be seen along the A32. Generations of Gosport people were born in the maternity hospital in Elson, which was also endowed by the Blakes family.

The Camper and Nicholson boatyards – now Endeavour Quay, adjacent to the Gosport Ferry Terminal – became world-famous yacht designers, particularly for the large J-Class yachts of the 1930s. And the area saw the ambitious development of Stokes Bay and Lee-on-the-Solent in the late nineteenth century as nouveau seaside resorts and desirable residential settlements.

As conservation officer at GBC, I have seen over seventy buildings added to the national register of listed buildings. This is primarily the result of Historic England carrying out detailed assessments of barracks, airfields, ordnance sites and hospitals. In addition, special cases worthy of inclusion are the Submarine Escape Training Tower in Blockhouse and the Second World War air-raid protection bunker on The Avenue. Gosport now has an extensive historic estate, with over 500 listed buildings, supplemented by eighteen conservation areas protecting key groups of buildings, historic village centres and several of the major military sites such as St George Barracks, *Daedalus*, Haslar and Priddy's Hard.

THE RESTORATION AND REPURPOSING IMPERATIVE

Gosport may be said to have 'thrived' during the Napoleonic Wars! The military legacy was significantly expanded with each subsequent conflict. However, following the bombing ravages of the Second World War and the civil demolition around the town centre in the 1950s, this process has reversed. From the 1980s, in particular, the scale of military withdrawal has meant that Gosport has had to begin to reinvent itself.

This comes with numerous challenges. The many military sites were generally served by sea and suffer from poor road access. They were also built for specific historic functions, with highly unusual buildings that are often difficult and costly to convert.

Gosport's discrete peninsular location, while it suited the military, does not make redevelopment easy. Land contamination, areas with depressed land values, the specialist skills required to convert listed buildings and

The pedestrianised High Street of Gosport, looking west from the ferry terminal. The High Street layout has changed numerous times since 1950 and is set to change again from 2022. (GP)

masterplan complex sites, the increasing risk of flooding (with sites needing significant investment to put in sea defences), nature conservation and environmental constraints, and an already densely populated urban area add to the challenges.

Below are some key examples of the challenges faced over the last twenty-five years as major sites have become available and where the importance of retaining the fabric of historic buildings and the sense of place inherent in an historic site has been at the centre of regeneration proposals. In other chapters of this book, you will find additional reference material for these iconic and indicative sites.

Royal Clarence Yard

Whenever a major site moves towards commercial release, the first priority is to avoid too much discussion until a thorough historic assessment of the site and its buildings has been completed. This key work, involving both historians and archaeologists, sets the basis of what really matters on a given site. With regard to Royal Clarence Yard, GBC commissioned a leading expert on military sites, Dr David Evans, to review a number of buildings, leading to the listing of several on the site.

Subsequent discussion ensured that there was a detailed archaeological management plan for the site, a thorough understanding of its historic development and, as individual buildings came forward for conversion, a recognition and record of their architectural and historic merits. The site

The past preserved. The impressive, centuries-old ceremonial gate into Flagstaff Green at Royal Clarence Yard. (GP)

The granary building and its massive, pillared under croft in Royal Clarence Yard. The under croft protected perishable cargoes as ships unloaded alongside. (GP)

was subject to an overall masterplan and it was agreed that it would be developed in detail in a number of self-contained phases.

With each phase, the local authority ensured that key historic buildings were repaired and commercial units were balanced against demands for residential use. In this way, for example, the restoration of the Cooperage came early in the phasing. Every building of historic interest has been preserved and converted to a new use and all development has been strictly controlled to ensure it respects the historic plan form of the site.

Sadly, while all the historic buildings were saved, the site still lacks the vitality envisaged for such an important mixed-use waterfront location. The biggest ongoing challenge has been securing commercial interest on a site with limited parking potential – a situation provoked by the developer securing at inquiry the right to significantly increase residential numbers at a time when local authorities were unable to secure parking standards.

St George Barracks

St George Barracks comprises a highly unusual series of linear barracks located just within the Gosport Lines and built following the Crimean War. The blocks north of Mumby Road were largely derelict in the late 1990s and the site south of Mumby Road, the location of the soldiers' barracks with its impressive colonnaded veranda, was closing down as a military site.

Detailed research and an archaeological assessment revealed some fascinating facts: perhaps most important was the clear defensive capability of the linear blocks as a 'last line of defence' were the ramparts ever to be breached. The flat roofs benefit from parapets at the perfect height for soldiers to fire over, and indeed enabled them to shoot over the ramparts themselves, providing extra covering fire. Furthermore, the western wall of the buildings was built thicker than the eastern; again, proof of its defensive capability were the Lines breached. While the flat roofs were initially intended to be earth covered, the buildings could not take the weight of the soil and this ability to utilise the roofs for defensive purposes was clearly a tactical bonus.

Once we understood all the historic buildings in detail and had a clear understanding of their layout, form, internal fittings and function, the conversions could go ahead. This was no easy task due to the terrible state of those alongside Weevil Lane, but eventually workable plans were provided by Berkeley Homes and Sunley Homes for all of the barracks to be successfully converted, although trying to fit modern housing standards into historic buildings with deep, vaulted flat roofs proved especially challenging.

Priddy's Hard

Released by the MoD in the late 1990s and taken on by the borough council with support from the county council, historic assessments identified this as the most significant ordnance depot in the UK and one of the best in the world for the range and extent of surviving historic buildings. Numerous listings followed.

The condition of several buildings was poor, but thanks to National Lottery Funding, urgent external works were undertaken and the north arm of the Camber Quay was reconstructed. The Millennium Project led to the addition of a bridge over Forton Lake, now a prominent Gosport landmark, as well as the conversion of the grade-I-listed Grand Magazine into Explosion: The Museum of Naval Firepower.

This novel and permanent exposition highlights the main functions of the provision of gunpowder and munitions to the Royal Navy. Similarly, the historic importance of the wider role of the site is indicated. It would have provided supplies during the American War of Independence, the great fleet actions of the Revolutionary and Napoleonic Wars, the arms race of the Dreadnought era and key supplies for every subsequent conflict up to the Falklands War of 1982.

While the core historic buildings were restored and in use, many were still vulnerable. The development by Crest Homes ensured some funding for residential building but did not address the restoration of several of the historic buildings. Funding was only recently secured through the Portsmouth Naval Base Property Trust, Historic England and the Heritage Lottery Fund. (The continuing story is taken up by Giles Pritchard in Chapter 11.) The need for external funding on a large scale for sites such as Priddy's Hard is symptomatic of the challenges the borough faces.

Royal Naval Hospital Haslar

The closure of the Royal Naval Hospital Haslar was of great local concern, and not just in terms of the loss of an excellent medical facility. The closure posed risks to the many historic buildings across the site. Soon after closure, as initial discussions were under way with the new owner, Our Enterprise Ltd, advice was sought from Charles Mynors, the leading authority on conservation law, as to which buildings on site should be regarded as listed. There were around a dozen or so named listed buildings at the time, but many ancillary buildings were not specifically referenced. His response was that every structure on site pre-dating 1947 (the date of the original planning act) should be regarded as listed; if not directly, then as 'curtilage' to the primary listed buildings ('curtilage' is a legal term referring to buildings that have an ancillary historic relationship to a primary listed building). This helped GBC negotiate from a strong position, not least because the grounds were also listed as a historic park.

With internal changes within Our Enterprise Ltd, negotiations were painfully slow. While buildings were secure and the site was reasonably well managed, no physical works took place for a decade beyond the conversion of the Officers' Terrace towards the south of the site, and the two pairs of officers' quarters flanking the facade to the main hospital. Nevertheless, detailed historic assessments and archaeological management plans were put in place and have ensured that now works have recommenced, which could be rolled out quite quickly.

Using a similar approach to that at Royal Clarence Yard, an overall outline consent was given, setting out the parameters for future phased development, and detailed applications have followed as each phase has been brought forward. Canada Block and G Block were delivered first, and now substantial works are under way to convert the southern range of the main hospital and to deliver a large underground car park within the quadrangle that will serve significant parts of future phases of the site. Sites such as Haslar take many years to deliver and it is hoped this will now move much more quickly to a satisfactory conclusion.

Gosport Railway Station

The Grade-II-listed Gosport Railway Station had been maintained as a ruin, much like a medieval abbey, since its closure in the 1960s. With repeated concern and pressure from the GBC, the owner, Hampshire County Council, agreed to put the site on the market to see if there was an opportunity to find a realistic viable use. In discussion with Guinness Homes, it was eventually agreed that the site had the potential to be converted into a mixed private/housing association development, with some live-work office accommodation included, and a community room.

The architects were ReFormat and they proposed to restore the original offices, while adding high-quality new build on the north side of the surviving wall to the northern platform. Additional discrete housing was located to the west, aligned with the northern platform. Additional works included the restoration of the former garden east of the offices and linking both platforms by reinstating the long-lost east and west facades to the original 1842 complex.

Although proving to be an expensive conversion, this multi-award-winning scheme has ensured the listed building will remain and while, sadly, this will not be as a railway station, it has been designed to respect the special character of this historic site.

Imaginative redesign. This modern housing complex appeared within the shell of the former Victorian railway station in Gosport. The station building had remained derelict for years after rail services were withdrawn. (LM)

Haslar Barracks

One recent success relates to the public support for the designation of Haslar Barracks as a conservation area. The former immigration holding centre was closed by the Ministry of Justice in 2017. The site had been on our radar for some time and being aware of the forthcoming closure, I carried out as much background research on the site as I could, helped by an extensive archive of historic maps gathered over many years.

With help from local historians, it became clear that the buildings on the site represented an almost unique survival of a barracks complex dating from around 1802. This was a regimental barracks, utilised by units assigned to defend Gosport in case of attack from France, and replaced tented encampments that had previously occupied the area. The buildings comprised single-storey barracks, a guardhouse, officers' quarters, a regimental hospital and various stores and ancillary buildings, all originally surrounded on three sides by walls and with a wall and railings to the south.

The waterfront had mooring facilities to embark and disembark troops, with ample space for parades within the enclosed grounds. A watercolour of the site dating from 1813 showed the buildings much as they appear today.

The site was converted soon after the Crimean War into a hospital for all Gosport garrison troops, with bed space for about 180 men and the addition of a covered walkway linking the wards (these being the former barrack buildings). Remarkably, the site remained little changed until its relatively recent use as a detention centre, and even then the form of the buildings and layout of the site remains intact.

It remains a question of debate as to whether some of the barrack buildings were rebuilt when it became a hospital, but even as a hospital complex it is a very early example of an army hospital at a pioneering phase in their development, influenced by Florence Nightingale's post-Crimean War recommendations. Prior to the mid-nineteenth century, the army dealt with sickness at regimental level and, other than the brief experiment of the military hospital at St Vincent's in Gosport around 1796, large-scale army hospitals simply did not exist.

The plan form is key to the significance of the site and this has been carefully detailed in the site's Conservation Area Appraisal (March 2018).

HERITAGE ACTION ZONES (HAZ) – CURRENT INITIATIVES

Historic England has provided substantial and financial support over recent years to restoration and redevelopment projects in the Gosport area, recognising the challenges faced by the town, its residents and GBC. This culminated in the creation of two HAZs – one looking to help invest in schemes across the borough, and one focused on the High Street and its extension, Stoke Road.

At the time of writing, the two local HAZ schemes have seen several businesses in the High Street and Stoke Road benefit from funding to upgrade their historic shopfronts and facades. Funds for conservation area reviews, appraisals and management plans for Stokes Bay, Alverstoke, Anglesey, the High Street, Stoke Road, Priddy's Hard and the Gosport Lines have also featured. Resources towards tree clearance and restoration works at Bastion No. 1 have been provided. Other supported work includes: Historic England LiDAR scanning the Gosport Trenches as a schools project; reviewing statutory designations in Blockhouse, HMS *Sultan* and Qinetiq Haslar Road; funds for viability assessments of the Wardroom in *Daedalus* and Fort Rowner; and projects to help develop heritage-led masterplans for Blockhouse and Haslar Barracks. There are also potential offers to help fund creative assessments on future uses for the vulnerable First World War seaplane hangars at *Daedalus*.

THE FUTURE

The approach of the GBC planning team has been to pro-actively understand and record the heritage value of sites across the area, with a process of dialogue in liaison with local historians and amenity groups. This enables negotiations with commercial developers from a position of strength – by having a detailed knowledge and understanding of the borough's built heritage. This knowledge can help to fast track realistic and practical schemes within clear principles for proposed new developments.

GBC has brought Historic England along in this process. While several key projects have been delivered, it is unquestionably the case that significant public sector investment is still likely to be required to ensure some especially complex buildings are secured for future generations.

There is plenty still to do in and around Gosport. Several sites require more detailed historic research. But, as someone central to the long process of conservation and restoration, I remain optimistic that through continued collaboration with local interest groups and key national bodies, the Gosport heritage will be secured and the area will gain the national visibility that it so justly deserves.

2

VANTAGE POINTS FROM THE VOLUNTARY SECTOR: THE GOSPORT SOCIETY PERSPECTIVE

Louis Murray

Founded just over fifty years ago, The Gosport Society is the local civic, history and amenity society for the Borough of Gosport. The society has registered-charity status and is a voluntary organisation for all those who are interested in and care about the built estate and the socio-geographical environment of Gosport. The formation and rise of the society was in no small measure a response and reaction to post-Second World War reconstruction and the large-scale demolition and urban renewal policies of the 1950s that tended to favour concrete, high-rise apartment buildings and uniform council estates – often at the expense of historically significant buildings that had managed to survive the conflagrations of war.

Gosport, like its cross-harbour neighbour Portsmouth, has long been associated with the defence of the realm. Portsmouth is often referred to as 'the home of the Royal Navy'. Similarly, Gosport makes claim to being the original home of HM Submarine Service of the Royal Navy.

A centuries-long maritime history and close association with the armed forces of the UK has helped to create a unique built estate that includes once-strategic fortifications, both onshore and offshore, in and around The Solent. It includes barracks and accommodation blocks that have attracted heritage listing for their architectural features and, in some cases, conversion to internationally reputable museums; military hospitals that have played a part in all of the twentieth-century wars that Britain has been involved in; relict survivors of Victorian and earlier Georgian and Regency houses and shops; 'Lines', or patterns of earth and brick ramparts and defence ditches that once surrounded the entire town; and airfields that witnessed the dawn of aviation and global events such the embarkation of the Allied forces on D-Day, 6 June 1944.

A bridge to the future. The Millennium Bridge over Forton Lake provides a splendid approach to the residential, leisure and museum group of buildings at Priddy's Hard. (LM)

A PATTERN OF CONTESTED DEVELOPMENT

Gosport suffered grievously in the Luftwaffe bombings of the Second World War. Military and civil buildings were damaged and destroyed; classic Georgian and Regency period facades were lost. Much of the High Street had to be rebuilt in the 1950s and 1960s.

This set a slow, uneven and contested pattern of urban renewal that, to this day, has never been fully reconciled to the wishes and aspirations of borough residents. In the first twenty years of the twenty-first century, the pattern continues to be one of struggle in the face of developers' vested interests, heightened citizen concerns for the preservation of buildings and locations of historic and architectural value, pressure from central government for ever more houses to be built as land banks shrink and brownfield sites become over-built, and frequently changing groups of councillors of GBC, who battle each other and grapple with policy formulation under conditions of tight municipal and financial stringency.

It is against such a backdrop that The Gosport Society came into being. Coupled with an abiding interest in the lives of noteworthy townspeople and residents and the growing perception of the need to conserve and repurpose buildings of architectural and historic merit, the society has come to

offer an additional 'democratic voice' to the people of Gosport and a partici-
patory arena outside the context of local elections, municipal bureaucracy,
local party politics and the commercially motivated development industry.
Simply put, The Gosport Society is the people's society!

A VOLUNTARY ORGANISATION

Voluntary organisations that have registered charity status usually operate
under a member-agreed constitution.* Such is the case with The Gosport
Society. Under the constitution, the formal objectives of The Gosport
Society are as follows:

- to educate and inform the public about Gosport's civic and social
  history, demographic and geographical character
- to promote and support high standards of town planning and architectural design in the built estate; especially in respect of designated
  conservation areas and listed buildings
- to secure the protection and preservation of historic buildings, gardens, public open spaces and sites of special scientific and cultural
  interest in the borough
- to promote research into the history and social development of the
  borough and to publish books and guides for the benefit of residents,
  tourists, research scholars and the cultural agents of the heritage
  industry such as Historic England and the Royal Society of Arts.

But How Does The Gosport Society Realise These Objectives?
By having a multistrand portfolio of actions! The interested reader can find
a full detailing of these actions in other associated publications (Murray,
2020). It is sufficient here to summarise an outline only.

In respect of town and municipal planning – a central implied theme of
this volume – the society prepares reports on how the urban environment
might be improved for the good of residents and visitors alike (see, for
example, 'Gosport Waterfront and Town Centre SPD Draft Consultation:
Gosport Society Response', 2017). Similarly, a 'privileged function' granted
to the society is that of commenting upon and, where required, objecting to
any formal planning application for building development in conservation

---

* The legal-rational status of The Gosport Society is further enhanced by codification of the
  financial regulations for 'good governance' from the Charities Commission.

Gosport's underused and outdated bus station is soon to be replaced with a new facility. A mixed-use waterfront development is promised for the site. (LM)

areas. To that end, the society maintains a planning subcommittee that, on a monthly basis, considers all received planning applications. In exercising this function, in dialogue with salaried officers of GBC, The Gosport Society has been instrumental in mediating (indeed, on occasions, stopping) the wilder ambitions of commercial property developers, who are often tempted to put profits before people. The archives of the society and the files of local newspapers reveal many examples where, down the years, old and often much-loved buildings have been saved from demolition.

GREEN PLAQUES

The Gosport Society is not anti-development. There is no imperative to keep historic buildings untouched and forever pickled in aspic. Rather, the society is wedded to the effective repurposing of buildings, whether that be for residential, commercial or public exhibitions, as for galleries and museums. The same predisposition applies to open spaces, as in the examples of the Alver Valley, the Stokes Bay proposed conservation area and the Browndown military training reserve. The imperative is that such repurposing should be done with due commitment to sensitive restoration of the fabric of historic buildings and application of modern conservation principles in the case of the natural environment.

In the case of historic buildings, the society devised a green plaque award scheme. This was instituted in 2011 to 'recognise and stimulate public interest in the high-quality restoration of historic buildings and structures in the borough'.

Owners of premises have been invited to nominate their properties where significant restoration work has been undertaken and completed. In allocating ceramic green plaques to six buildings (see below) in the borough, the society paid particular attention to the following nomination criteria:

- the historical significance of the nominated building
- the importance of the building to broader questions of heritage
- the architectural merits of the existing structure
- the uniqueness or exceptionality of the existing structure
- the synthesis of the restoration plan with the original form and character of the building
- the quality of the workmanship deployed in the restoration
- the quality of the materials used in the restoration
- the enhanced amenity and/or aesthetic value of the restoration to the Gosport community.

The currently empty, formidable-looking Haslar Barracks has had many occupiers and its Georgian architecture and structure remains largely intact – an enduring model of its time. (LM)

Representatives of Hampshire County Council, the Gosport Society, Historic England, Gosport Borough Council and the Defence Infrastructure Organisation sign the Heritage Action Zone (HAZ) Partnership Agreement in the Old Grammar School on 11 June 2019. (GBC)

No. 5 Grange Farm, Alver Valley

Dating from manorial times, this historic property has long been considered to be an exemplar of the criteria listed above. The details of the restoration and something of the history of Grange Farm are outlined in Chapter 9.

Royal Engineers Mews, Weevil Lane

Part of the former garrison of Gosport, opposite the imposing colonial-style former St George Barracks, itself redeveloped into a series of modern apartments, this collection of workshop blocks, stables and storehouses has been converted into a series of stylish dwellings that add to the range and variety of the accommodation stock in Gosport.

Church Cottage, Rowner Lane

Adjacent to the ancient Church of St Mary the Virgin, Rowner, the only grade-I-listed church in the borough, the cottage remains one of very few traditional thatched houses still to be found in the town.

Gosport Old Railway Station, Spring Garden Lane
The word 'iconic' may be overused in heritage and conservation circles, but the old railway station building certainly merits that title. In a prominent position on the corner of Spring Garden Lane and Mumby Road, it is arguably the most visible and publicly recognised Victorian facade in the town. Its place in the railway history of Gosport is featured in Chapter 10.

The Superintendent's House, Royal Clarence Yard
Dating from 1830, this house is one of several restored buildings facing inwards into Flagstaff Green, the ornamental square that lies just inside the monumental main gate that once opened to Weevil Lane, at the former Royal Navy victualling depot of Royal Clarence Yard.

The Bakery, Royal Clarence Yard
This large building, imposingly facing the Semaphore Tower in HM Dockyard across Portsmouth Harbour, was once one of the most functional of the many single-purpose buildings in Royal Clarence Yard. The preserved ovens, which once turned out ships biscuits by the ton in the days of sail, are a striking internal feature of the restoration.

HERITAGE IN URBAN AND PUBLIC OPEN SPACES

Gosport is short of public open spaces. The 9,765 square miles of the Gosport peninsula, approximating to the local government boundaries, is more than 80 per cent urbanised. Within living memory, large tracts of former farmland at sites such as Rowner, Bridgemary and the Cheque Farm estate to the west of the Alver River have been resumed for large-scale house building and commercial development. Ditto, land released by the Ministry of Defence at the *Daedalus* site (Solent Airport), in Lee-on-the-Solent, and around the former munitions depot of Priddy's Hard.

The Gosport population of 82,662 (2011 Census) is primarily a population of town dwellers. While the town has some fine parks and an 18-mile waterfront (sections of which are access-restricted under the terms of the Official Secrets Act), which includes Stokes Bay, lately proposed as a new conservation area, open spaces for outdoor recreation, particularly north of Stoke Road and along the line of the A32, are at a premium.

Pot luck. The Alver Valley Garden Centre opened in March 2022, heralding a new era of commercial and social rejuvenation of historic lands to the west of Gosport town centre adjacent to Grange Farm. (LM)

However, fragments of former natural woodland can be found at Oakdene Wood and Rowner Copse; foreshore nature reserves can be found in isolated pockets such as Monks Walk and at Elmore in Lee-on-the-Solent; coastal heathland can be found around Fort Gilkicker and in the Ministry of Defence (MoD) training reserve north of Privett Road; and the Alver Valley Country Park is a splendid green lung between the built-up area of Gosport and Lee-on-the-Solent. These precious spaces act to accentuate the unique geography of Gosport.

Massive Palmerstonian fortresses dating from the 1860s rub shoulders with post-Second World War housing estates. Former Ministry of Defence structures and installations have found new life as residences and retail complexes. Tightly packed streets of Victorian and Edwardian terraced houses spatially define and dictate traffic flows in districts such as Elson and Forton. Elegant Regency and Georgian style mansions, often in ornate garden settings, yield pleasing-to-the-eye vistas and a 'village feel' in Alverstoke and Anglesey.

Art deco and post-modern villas form discrete architectural enclaves in Lee-on-the-Solent. These latter contrast markedly with the serial modern-day imperative of large-scale housing projects in Identikit, municipally dictated incarnations at Bridgemary, constructed for more than 25,000 people (nearly a third of the entire population of Gosport) on lands sequestered in the 1940s from feudal owners (Prideaux-Brune estates) whose lineage dates back to the twelfth century. Ditto, in their early twenty-first-century garden suburb, the high-density concentration model at Cherque Farm, Priddy's Hard and the euphemistically named Alver Village at Rowner.

WALKABOUTS AS AN ACTIVE HERITAGE STRATEGY

The Gosport Society has chosen a strategy of 'active walking' to construe urban and open-space geography from a heritage and social history stand-point in Gosport. Four trails guides were produced from 2013 onward to enable visitors and residents alike to walk in and among locations of inter-est and to learn their backstories. They are (in date of publication order):

- The Gosport Town Trail (2013)
- Curious Encounters in Gosport Parks and Gardens (2014)
- Putting People in Their Places: Gosport Worthies and Whereabouts in Times of Tumult, Talent and Transformation (2016)
- Naval Gazing in Gosport: Nautical Nooks Worth Prying For (2017).

These pocket-size, full-colour booklets embrace the concept of 'freedom walking'. People are encouraged to wander at will, in their own time and at their own pace, to learn about and embrace heritage by seeking out unusual architectural and landscape features, to adopt an enquiring mind about changes to the pattern of land use over time, to come to know the history of buildings and the people that utilised them, and to encounter the animal and plant life in parks, gardens and local nature reserves.

The success of these booklets in reaching large numbers of people over a ten-year period and satisfying a thirst for local knowledge and storytell-ing was in no small measure a catalyst for the production and publication in 2021 of a fully illustrated comprehensive walking guide to Gosport and its next-door neighbour, Fareham. This book addressed part of the Historic England agenda for HAZs – a national programme designed to raise aware-ness of the built estate in places with a long history, such as Gosport and Ramsgate. See L. Murray, *20 Historic Walks in Gosport and Fareham* (LDJ Educational in association with The Gosport Society, 2021).

Heritage is a state of mind as well as a visible historical legacy in the town-scape. For many years, Gosport has had an image problem. Concern has been expressed by voluntary sector agencies and GBC about indifferent and negative portrayals of the town as 'the poor relation of Portsmouth'.

Negative imagery has negative consequences. These may include low morale among residents, limited spending in the High Street, low inward investment to boost employment, laissez-faire attitudes to the impact of the reduction of the traditional armed forces presence, and an indifference to the 800-year political and cultural history of the town.

Times change. People are not cultural dopes. They aspire. They take an interest when given the opportunity. They live in times of enhanced interest in the natural environment. They better perceive the significance of what is around them and what is happening to them. They want to exercise a measure of control over their lives. They perhaps latently realise that 'opportunity' is all around but needs to be first perceived then firmly grasped.

In 2021 there is a sense of urgency tempered by cautious optimism in planning for Gosport's future. As well as the municipal authority (GBC), there are agencies in the public and private spheres in active debate about alternative socioeconomic futures for Gosport.

This 'urgency' is not only mirrored in council debates – where it might be expected to, and does, form a running and recurrent narrative. It is also a driver in the activities of the Solent Local Enterprise Partnership, The Gosport Society, the Defence Infrastructure Organisation (DIO), the Arts Council (South-East), the Hampshire Cultural Trust and the Hampshire County Council. Indeed, the latter four entities are now in a partnership designed to enact the ideals of the HAZ status accorded in 2019 to Gosport by Historic England, the statutory authority most centrally committed under government policies to rejuvenate deserving places such as Gosport. This central government part-funded initiative plans to inject new life, new people, new uses and new meanings into sites such as Bastion No. 1, Fort Blockhouse, the Gunboat Yard, Priddy's Hard, the Old Grammar School and other sites.*

For a more expanded listing of Gosport projects under the HAZ branding by Historic England, see R. Cook, 'Heritage Action Zone: A Gosport Milestone for the Future' in *Gosport 2020: For the Record – Essays in Celebration of the Half-Centenary of The Gosport Society* (2020).

---

* For further exposition, go to www.thinkingplace.co.uk.

'Thinking Place', or 'The Gosport Perceptions Study', is an ongoing initiative to provide a storyboard for the trends described in the above paragraph. Thinking Place is actually an independent urban consultation agency. It specialises in construing towns, boroughs and villages as 'ideas of mind' as well as geographical entities. Commissioned by GBC, Thinking Place consulted widely about the town in 2019–20. Its 'Grand Tour' question is of the type 'What do you think about Gosport?'

Answers to this question permitted Thinking Place to produce a visually illustrated, computerised schemata and also a large-print book of striking graphic design called *Gosport's Story*, which tells of Gosport as it is, what people think of it, and what it might become if focused investment is able to capitalise on its heritage. Thinking Place uses abstract formulations to attract inward investment by illuminating 'possibility' in the mortar and fabric of the town.

The approach has apparently met with some success in Coventry, Hull, Knowsley and other UK towns and cities. So – for Thinking Place – Gosport is a location where the following five symbolic themes emerge, to give meaning, purpose and possibility for the town and its people:

- 'Water – or Deep Blue Celebration'
- 'Fighting for a Share of Mind – Re-Imagining and Reanimating History'
- 'Wearing a Coat Covering Many Treasures'
- 'The Environment for Fresh Thinking – Making Place the Hero'
- 'Gosport – Our Growth is Natural and New'

There you have it! These themes from 2020 onwards should translate into a form of civic pride and belief in Gosport that The Gosport Society has long advocated.

There is much that is unique and admirable about Gosport's heritage. But the town cannot stand still. It cannot bask in former glories, whatever they might have been. Heritage, conservation and social and economic rejuvenation are, in 2022, perceived to be most definitely not mutually exclusive. A future drawn out of the long history of Gosport beckons: new industrial and employment opportunities; an enhanced and energised cultural and social environment; an easy and relaxed living space for residents; a restored but working built estate that acknowledges history and continues to act as a beacon of legitimate pride in what Gosport was, what Gosport is, and what it will look like in the future.

3

HERITAGE OPEN DAYS (HODS): ACCESS FOR THE UNDERSTANDING OF LOCAL HISTORY

Sue Courtney and Louis Murray

The month of September each year in the UK witnesses a series of events for the public that have become known as Heritage Open Days (HODs). They typically include the opening to view of historic buildings and heritage sites that are not normally accessible to the general public. The HODs movement has grown over more than twenty-five years to become a significant fixture in the cultural and tourist calendar.

The Tourist Information Centre adjacent to the Gosport Ferry Terminal. It is the epicentre for Heritage Open Days and is often a first point of call for heritage visitors to Gosport. (GP)

European Heritage Days began in 1991 in mainland Europe as an initiative by the Council of Europe and the European Commission to highlight the rich and diverse cultural assets of Europe. They allowed public access to historic monuments and buildings normally closed to the public.

In 1992, two years before the national HODs were officially launched in the UK, Gosport, the so-called 'little town with the big history', participated in the first pilot events. The Civic Trust, an influential body primarily interested in the preservation of the built estate in the UK, also lent its influence to the momentum for a nationwide festival. Lesley Burton, a member of the Civic Trust for South-East England at that time, was inspired to take on the initiative in Gosport.

Peter Chegwin, then leader of GBC, was enthusiastic about the concept, offering council support. However, it was the independent local voluntary organisation and civic society – The Gosport Society – then in its twentieth year of existence, that took on the responsibility of organising events. This effectively represented the start of England's contribution to European heritage festivals.

Rival activity also took place in towns and cities elsewhere in the UK. Indeed, Berwick-upon-Tweed, with its long history of Anglo-Scottish border

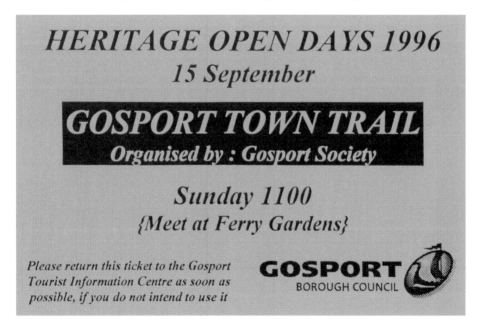

An urban walk called the 'Gosport Town Trail' featured on this now-historic ticket for the 1996 Heritage Open Days programme. (BP)

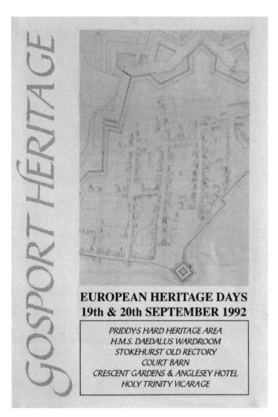

wars, opened its ramparts as another pilot event in 1992. A friendly and jocular dialogue has persisted with Gosport ever since as to which town got in first. No matter! HODs now has its own organisational structure and has gone on to become arguably England's largest festival of history, heritage and culture.

Lesley Burton, a stalwart and advocate of The Gosport Society, had thought that the 'HODs idea' would be popular. She believed people would be curious about their local history and, if prompted and guided, they would come out in significant numbers to look anew at what was around them. Many residents were aware of the existence of historic sites in their midst but were less aware of the vitally important role they have played in UK history over the centuries.

Thus, on 19–20 September 1992, a foundation European Heritage Days programme offered access to the Priddy's Hard heritage area; the Wardroom at HMS *Daedalus* in Lee-on-the-Solent; the Stokehurst Old Rectory on Anglesey Road; the ancient but preserved agricultural property of Court Barn off Broom Way in Lee-on-the-Solent; the Crescent Gardens and Anglesey Hotel in Alverstoke; and the vicarage of the Holy Trinity Church in central Gosport.

A printed programme for the two days is preserved in The Gosport Society archives (see illustration on p38). Following the event, this extract from The Gosport Society Newsletter of December 1992 indicates a vindication of society thinking:

> European Heritage Days. This event proved a great success and judging from the many letters was warmly appreciated by members of the public who were able to visit many establishments normally unavailable. It was a joint effort with the borough council who organised the ticket distribution and linked the leaders – in turn members of the Society were most co-operative and their willingness to act as volunteers during the two days ensured the complete success of the venture. This has put Gosport firmly 'on the map' in Strasbourg.

BEYOND STRASBOURG!

Early HODs events were primarily weekends only. The first and the most popular places to open were both active and former MoD sites. These included the Georgian victualling facility for the Royal Navy at Royal Clarence Yard; the munitions and gunpowder depot at Priddy's Hard; and the 200-year-old plus Royal Naval Hospital Haslar.

On the first opening, visits were restricted to two or three tours in a day and ten to twelve people per tour, for reasons of manageability. However, Lesley Burton remembers people gathering at the gates of some sites begging to be let in. One visitor burst into tears during the tour of Priddy's Hard. His mother had worked there but had never told her son how important her work was because she wasn't allowed to under the terms of the Official Secrets Act – a proscription that applied to many citizens working in and around the various military installations in Gosport.

A flavour of HODs early days is gleaned from this extract from the minutes of a meeting of The Gosport Society held on Wednesday, 28 April 1999 at the home of the honorary secretary, Beryl Peacey of 2a Bentham Road, Alverstoke:

> Heritage Sites for 11/12 September 1999. The Chairman and Honorary Secretary reported on a recent meeting with Michael Nutt and Ms P. Grey of the Tourist Information when possible sites were discussed. It was generally agreed that the following sites might

be made available – subject to MoD approval and co-operation. 1. Royal Clarence Yard. 2. Royal Hospital Haslar. 3. Fort Blockhouse. 4. DERA and Gunboat Yard. 5. Fort Rowner. 6. St George Barracks South. 7. Fort Gilkicker. With the two walks of Alverstoke and High Street Gosport. There would be the vintage bus service and the possibility of Number 2 Battery – in which there would be an Aviation Display this summer. The Honorary Secretary reminded members that she would need volunteers as usual to help steward these events. There would be a further meeting on 25 May when these sites would be finalised.

HODS EVENTS PROGRAMMES

HODs events in Gosport cover major aspects of the town's history and heritage. These range from the army occupancy of Fort Brockhurst to talks about the former Grange Airfield (now a Royal Navy engineering facility known as HMS *Sultan*); from guided walks in parks and memorial gardens,

Curiosities – a visitor to HODs could expect to see many unusual sights around town. These Second World War anti-tank obstacles, previously guarding Fort Brockhurst, were moved with the active participation of the Gosport Society to Brockhurst Gate, a typical and modern out-of-town retail park. (LM)

such as the Hermitage Wildlife Garden and Anns Hill Old Cemetery, to tours of active science and engineering works, such as the Institute of Naval Medicine at Alverstoke and the ship-testing tanks of the Qinetiq Marine Technology Park at Haslar. There are also family-friendly workshops, poetry and photographic competitions (see below), street theatre, readings in public libraries, pop-up exhibitions of local craft wares and heritage quizzes at local pubs.

Statistics collected each year suggest that many visitors return year after year. Attendance at events often encourages people to find out more about their local heritage and take a pride in their local history.

Visitors are not just local but come from all parts of the UK and beyond. Indeed, HODs may be said to have become a commercially significant tourist attraction in their own right. The internet and new digital and social media facilities now make HODs programmes accessible as virtual advertising and publicity events to pretty much anywhere in the world.

PROGRESS

Gosport HODs have grown over the years, both in the number of events available and the number of visitors attending these events. Terry Rhodes, the current chair of the Gosport HODs organisation, has been generous in the information and support given in the writing of this chapter. She has shared some interesting statistics:

- In 2009, six events were held, attracting 970 visitors.
- By 2017, the offering had grown to eighty-nine events, of which forty-seven were new, attracting 14,993 visitors.
- In 2018, there were seventy-six events, of which twenty-three were new, attracting 16,701 visitors.
- Due to Covid restrictions, 2020 was the first year when serious digital content was used to replace and/or augment actual in-person visiting. Twenty-nine events were offered, of which fourteen were new. They attracted 12,822 'visitors', many of which were online viewings.
- In 2021, there were sixty-nine events, including thirty-four that were new, attracting 16,436 visitors inclusive of digital viewings.

THE ORGANISATION OF HODS

Gosport HODs are organised by a team of independent local volunteers who function as an administrative secretariat. This team meets periodically throughout the year in convenient venues such as Elson Community Hub Library. Their key organisational premise is to offer a varied programme of largely unique events, giving the public opportunities to see hidden places and explore new experiences – and all for free.

Local experts lead the walks and talks. Much of the preparatory and booking work is undertaken through the highly visible Tourist Information Centre, adjacent to the Gosport Ferry Terminal. A heavy footfall in this location means that publicity, information and ticketing is advantaged.

A second organisation premise is that of accessibility. Gosport is known to

COURT BARN

The Court Barn Conservative Club now occupies this 16th. century farmhouse, which was one of the most important buildings in the local area in medieval times. It was held by many significant local families who oversaw the surrounding common tenants and  smallholders on behalf of the Lords of the Manor of Lee Breton. Inside this timber-framed building, the main hall, inglenook fireplace, 'secret' staircase and large unvaulted cellars still remain.

Guided tours at: 11.00am, 1.00pm & 3.00pm Saturday only
Car parking available at: Conservative Club car park, Court Barn Lane, off Broom Way, Lee-on-the-Solent

HOLY TRINITY VICARAGE

Surrounded by the 17th Century De Gomme defensive fortifications, this former Commander's House stands as a lonely reminder of the Georgian old town of Gosport which was badly damaged by wartime bombing. The Vicarage and Church have interesting historical connections with the novelist Jane Austen, the composer George Frederick Handel and the locally notorious Bingham family! The Holy Trinity Church will also be open as usual on this weekend.

Guided tours at:
Saturday 10.00am, 12.00pm, 2.00pm & 4.00pm
Sunday 2.00pm & 4.00pm
Car parking available at:
Trinity Green & Town Centre car parks

Court Barn, in Lee-on-the-Solent, and Holy Trinity Vicarage, in central Gosport, were places for public visiting in the inaugural 1992 European Heritage Days. (BP)

run the most accessible HODs events in the country. From the beginning of the annual planning stage, Terry Rhodes and her team consider the diverse range of people who may wish to enjoy events and what their physical and mobility needs might be. Guides are offered disability awareness training. Walks for differing levels of ability are considered, including the provision for people on mobility scooters. Audio-visual elements and facilities for those with sensory impairments are included as well as quiet weekday events for visitors who prefer small groups. A distinctively coloured, pocket-sized paper programme outlines bus links, wheelchair and buggy suitability and accessible toilet access. Much use is made of the distinctive 'H' symbol to indicate the what, when and where of HODs week.

COVID 19 AND BEYOND: THE NEED TO RETHINK PRESENTATION AND VISITATION PROTOCOLS

Legal restrictions caused by the Covid pandemic led to a detailed recon-sideration of how the format of HODs might be subject to changes in the future. In particular, thought has been given to how Gosport HODs might make better use of advances in technology to extend programme offerings.

The possibility of having video tours of venues with limited physical capac-ity is one opportunity. This could enable more people to attend virtually. The organisers of HODs are also mindful of the possible future for the burgeoning heritage industry. This might include engagement with new interests in the ecology of architecture; the regeneration of craft skills in areas such as stone-masonry, landscape painting, patchwork and lace-making.

A borough-wide Gosport Cultural Compact – recently adopted as policy by GBC – offers a potential integrated framework that HODs can continue to prosper within. Ditto, the rejuvenation of historical locations under the Historic England HAZ programme.

A model for HODs to extend their focus can be seen at the former muni-tions and gunpowder factory at Priddy's Hard. This once-prohibited place has emerged from semi-dereliction to house an internationally significant museum (Explosion – The Museum of Naval Firepower), an imaginative pub restaurant (the Powder Monkey) built inside a former gunpowder maga-zine, a conserved Georgian harbour (the Camber); and a rebuilt promenade up to the Hardway conservation area, providing magnificent views across Portsmouth Harbour. The ramparts of Priddy's Hard, buried for years under matted vegetation, are now re-emerging to view and in a few years will make a superb walkway and linear public park around the moated parts of the site.

THE WIDER PERSPECTIVE

HODs could extend on to perhaps the less-fashionable areas or lesser-known parts of the borough. The Alver Valley Country Park, still in development, has many 'secrets' to explore, including Noah Lake, the Wildgrounds and a seventeenth-century village. The Rowner and Bridgemary areas offer for exploration local nature reserves such as Oakdene Wood and child-friendly Bridgemary Park. Lee-on-the-Solent has its emblematic art deco enclave in Milvil Road. The community orchard in Leesland Park abutting the former railway 'triangle' is well worth visiting for fruit pickings, scented perambulations along the sensory trail and sighting the location of a long forgotten but once vital industry – the Victorian and Edwardian steam laundry. And in the old district of Elson, towards the end of Ham Lane, the intriguing story of the Blake maternity hospital (now converted into residences and where generations of 'Gosporteers' were born) awaits rediscovery by the local population born elsewhere! Other possibilities on the drawing board include the use of QR codes for mobile phones when outside a building or structure, which can reveal and permit access to historical resources such as old photos and important facts relating to the building and the area in which it stands.

PHOTOGRAPHIC COMPETITIONS

In 2018, HODs initiated its first-ever photographic competition. Local man Jason Brodie-Browne was the fitting winner of this competition with his unusual view of Haslar Hospital. There were over 300 submissions featuring places of every age, style and purpose. The judges were Matt Emmett, Historic Photographer of the Year 2017 and author of *Forgotten Heritage*, and Andy Henderson, HODs social media and photography production manager. Andy commented on the image:

> For me, Jason's photo really communicates one of the best things about Heritage Open Days, the ability to venture behind usually closed doors and discover a different side to your local heritage. This is a well thought-out, clever image that has a real sense of mystery and intrigue. A worthy winner of our first photography competition.

Giving his reasons for taking this particular photograph, Jason said:

> The winning image I shot came as a complete surprise to me! Since the hospital closed in 2007 the site has always been a place of interest for photographers as it slowly decayed. I spent a lot of my youth around the hospital as both my parents worked there. This being the case, it holds a lot of memories.
>
> Although the closure and subsequent decay was extremely sad and difficult for the area, I thought it was important to record it photographically. The photo I thought looks quite dark and sinister, which may reflect the countless lives lost within the walls of the hospital but also possibly shows a part of the hospital that was essential to life there.
>
> Walking around an area like Haslar is difficult as access is limited. This scene caught my eye for that very reason. Barred from prying eyes with the plaque on the door stating 'Hazardous', it also created a scene of intrigue and danger. I tried to keep the wire fencing in the foreground to show this. Knowing that many of these scenes will soon be gone forever, capturing views such as this in camera is the reason why I choose to attend GHOD events.

INTRIGUE, HAZARD, DANGER?

All are ingredients in the HODs salad. All are likely to capture the imagination. All are likely to motivate. They could even be a motif for what HODs is all about. Somebody once said, 'The past is another country'. Well, other 'countries' are well worth visiting! The future may also be 'another country' – one full of potential, the opportunity for discovery and for a better understanding of what we as a people are about. And that is truly what HODs is committed to. Keeping Our Island Story alive for generations to come.

4

BURY HOUSE: ARCHITECTURE, REDEVELOPMENT AND RESIDENCE OVER TIME

Malcolm Stevens

INTRODUCTION

Bury House is situated on the north side of Bury Road, approximately 1 mile west of Gosport town centre. Over the years, thousands of people have driven or walked past the Georgian mansion without giving it a second glance. Many local inhabitants will have been familiar with the building through their involvement with the Gosport Community Association (GCA), of which it now forms the administrative centre, but will be unaware of the story of this once-grand home and its illustrious residents.

The hamlet of Bury, or Berry, as it was previously known, is one of the oldest settlements on the Gosport peninsula, dating back to the thirteenth century. If we were able to travel back in time some 300 years, we would discover a cluster of farmhouses and farm workers' cottages located at the intersection of two quiet country lanes with dwellings along the southern section (now The Avenue) leading to the village of Alverstoke, and several cottages scattered along the eastern section (now Bury Road), leading to the town of Gosport. The hamlet was surrounded by cultivated fields with views across to those larger settlements, The Solent and Portsmouth Harbour.

Set back along that eastern lane, we would have noticed some building activity with a three-storey red-brick mansion rising from the ground. Bury House was to become the largest dwelling in the area and an engraved brick discovered near the eaves confirms its date of construction as 1720.

Bury House's frontage and the garden in which Mary Ann South (1817–1910) and her father conducted a notorious book burning. (BP)

Bury House has changed greatly over the centuries. New extensions have been added and later removed but the central house stands as it did on completion. The earliest description discovered is from a newspaper of 1788, advertising the sale of:

> … a desirable freehold estate called Berry House, consisting of a handsome and substantial brick dwelling-house, three stories high, and containing four good rooms on a floor, neatly fitted up, with convenient cellars, wine vaults, brewhouse, coach house, stabling for six horses and various other offices, all well-watered and in complete repair, large gardens in great perfection, planted with the choicest fruit trees, a rookery, and thirty acres of very fine land adjoining.

JOHN HATCH

The original owners of Bury House were merchant John Hatch and his wife, Margaret. A legal document exists that indicates John Hatch was already living on the land he owned at Bury a year before the house was constructed. This suggests that it may have been a replacement for an earlier dwelling on the site.

The restored Music Room in Bury House is the location for diverse cultural events. (BP)

As well as the 'convenient cellars and wine vaults' described in the above newspaper, the inclusion of an easily accessed rooftop lookout position indicates that the original house had a second purpose to that of providing a home for Hatch and his family. This came to light when uncovering a parliamentary document from 1733; a report of a committee of the House of Commons appointed to inquire into 'the Frauds and Abuses in the Customs'. It identified that John Hatch was one of the main smugglers operating along the Hampshire coast. There were several descriptions of running contraband ashore at Stokes Bay and in Portsmouth Harbour near Elson and taking them to his vaults at Berry.

John Hatch was eventually captured and tried for smuggling in 1725 and sent to the Fleet, a debtor's prison in London. He was finally released in 1733 on payment of a fine of £2,500, a considerable sum of money at the time. The assumption is that Hatch sold Bury House to Peter Solgard in that year, in order to raise the money to secure his release. However, it is likely that Solgard had been renting Bury House for some years previous, enabling Hatch to support himself and his family while incarcerated in Fleet Prison.

PETER SOLGARD

According to the eighteenth-century *Biographia Navalis*, Captain Peter Solgard was 'a gentleman of foreign extraction, we believe Danish'. Naval records indicate that having been promoted captain in the Royal Navy in 1722, his first commission was on HMS *Greyhound*, stationed off the New England Coast. On 10 June 1723, his ship engaged two pirate vessels off Delaware Bay, the *Fortune* and the *Ranger*, captained respectively by the notorious Edward Low and Charles Harris.

Although the *Fortune* escaped, Solgard captured the *Ranger* and its crew. The *Greyhound* then returned to Newport, Rhode Island, where Harris and thirty-five crew members were put on trial a month later. Most of the pirates were convicted and hanged in what remains one of the largest mass executions in the history of America.

At the time, the citizens along the east coast of America were plagued with the activities of pirates and when Solgard returned triumphantly to New York less than a week after the historic execution, the grateful Corporation of New York granted Captain Solgard the Freedom of the City. He was presented with a gold snuffbox, engraved with the city arms on one side and a picture of the *Greyhound*'s fight with the pirate sloops on the other.

Over the next fifteen years, Solgard moved from ship to ship and by 1737 he was captain of HMS *Berwick*, the Portsmouth guard ship. The following year, the *Berwick* sailed for the Mediterranean and shortly after arriving in Gibraltar, Peter Solgard died of a fever and was buried there. His will, signed before his departure, left Bury House and his estate to his cousin, Lieutenant Samuel Marshall.

SAMUEL MARSHALL SENIOR

For the next sixty years, Bury House was in the ownership of the Marshall family. Samuel Marshall Senior began his naval career as an ordinary seaman on board HMS *Greyhound*, captained by Peter Solgard. By 1747 he had been promoted to captain and was in command of the ill-fated HMS *Namur* on the East Indies station.

On 13 April 1749, the *Namur* floundered 90 miles south of Madras. Marshall was saved, but 520 of the crew died.

In 1758, while commanding HMS *Nottingham*, Samuel Marshall was involved in the Siege of Louisburg as part of the Seven Years' War, which ended the French colonial era in Atlantic Canada. Then, in 1762, he took part

The fascinatingly geometric stairwell in Bury House, leading to the nooks and crannies typical of houses of the period. (BP)

in operations against Martinique. His *Biographia Navalis* entry concludes, 'We do not know him to have held any commission after the conclusion of the war nor indeed have we any other particulars concerning him, except that he died at Gosport in the month of April 1768.'

He was buried at St Mary's Church, Alverstoke. His widow, Edith, continued to live at Bury House until she died in January 1784, when ownership passed to her son, also Samuel Marshall.

PEREGRINE HOPSON

An advertisement in the *Hampshire Telegraph* in 1759 reveals that the Marshall family rented Bury House out for a period while Samuel Marshalls senior and junior were both serving on HMS *Nottingham* in North America: 'To let, Berry House. 4 rooms to a floor, with brewhouse and laundry over at Berry [...] late in the occupation of General Hopson deceased.'

Further reference to the tenure of General Peregrine Hopson can be found in the *Dictionary of Canadian Biography* (University of Toronto), 'Hopson in his will, drawn up a month before he left for Martinique, had provided for a niece, Lydia Goodall, who was living with him at Berry, near Gosport, Hampshire.'

General Peregrine Hopson (1696–1759) was a British Army officer who commanded the 40th Regiment of Foot, saw extensive service and rose to the rank of major general. He played a significant role in the development of English Nova Scotia, served as British Commander in Louisbourg during the British occupation between 1746–49, and then became Governor of Nova Scotia in 1752.

After returning from Nova Scotia in 1755, he took up residence in Bury House. He was promoted major general in 1757 and once the Seven Years' War broke out, Hopson returned to Halifax with army reinforcements and helped organise the British response to the threat of a French attack.

The following year, Hopson was selected to lead an expedition to the West Indies by King George II. There, Hopson contracted a tropical disease and died on 27 February 1759 in Guadeloupe.

SAMUEL MARSHALL JUNIOR

Samuel Marshall Junior was born in Bury House and his baptism is recorded at St Mary's Church, Alverstoke, on 7 March 1741. He started his naval career in 1753 as a servant to his father, then captain of HMS *Tiger*. He rose through the ranks and was promoted captain in 1771. By that time, he had married Elizabeth Worsley, daughter of Sir Edward Worsley of Gatcombe, Isle of Wight.

His claim to fame is as the captain of the frigate HMS *Arethusa* and the action that occurred on 17 June 1778 off the coast of Brest in France. He is described in the *Naval Atalantis* as 'the officer who struck the first blow last war [...] *Arethusa* engaged the French ship, *La Belle Poule*, thereby commencing hostilities between Great Britain and France'. It was depicted as a David versus Goliath Battle of the *Arethusa*, 'a stumpy little frigate, scanty in crew, light in guns', against *La Belle Poule*, described as 'a splendid ship, with heavy metal, and a crew more than twice as numerous as that of the tiny *Arethusa*'. Both ships were badly damaged in the engagement but survived to fight another day.

In July 1788, the *Hampshire Chronicle* carried an advertisement announcing the sale by auction of Bury House. Samuel Marshall was moving to London to become Commissioner of Victualling for the Royal Navy. In 1794, he was promoted to Deputy Controller of the Navy and in the same year was knighted by King George III during a royal visit to the ships at Spithead. Sir Samuel Marshall died at his house in Cavendish Square, London, on 2 October 1795, aged 55.

THOMAS ATKINSON SENIOR

Ownership of Bury House eventually passed to solicitor Thomas Atkinson in August 1791. Thomas was engaged as a naval agent, dealing with the distribution of prize money ensuing as the spoils of war to the crew of Royal Naval ships. At the beginning of 1794, his wife Hannah gave birth to a son named after his father, and several months later, Thomas signed his last will and testament, leaving his estate at Bury to his wife and then to his son on reaching the age of 21 years. Thomas Atkinson died the following year and Hannah and her infant son moved to a property in North Street, Gosport.

For the next fourteen years, Bury House was leased, firstly to Thomas Whitear from 1795–1800, then farmer Cornelius Hayter 1800–11, John Atkinson (probably a relative of the owners) 1812–13 and finally Charles Finch, 1814–19.

CHARLES FINCH

An advertisement in the *Hampshire Telegraph* in June 1814 signifies a change of use for Bury House. Headed 'Asylum for Persons afflicted with Mental Derangement established at BERRY HOUSE, near Gosport', it describes that the house had been:

A traditional vestibule of many doors, the one on the left giving access to a community restaurant. (BP)

… fitted up in superior style, at a great expense for the reception of patients of the first respectability afflicted with Mental Derangement, under the immediate care and superintendence of Mr And Mrs C. Finch, who for many years have devoted their whole time and attention to alleviate the sufferings of those intrusted to their care.

Charles Finch and his wife only lived at Bury House until August 1819, when they set up a similar establishment at Fisherton-Anger in Wiltshire.

THOMAS ATKINSON JUNIOR

Thomas Atkinson Junior inherited Bury House in 1815 on his 21st birthday. He had married three years earlier, when both he and his wife Elizabeth were minors. Indeed, if Elizabeth's age recorded at subsequent censuses was accurate then she was just 12 years old at the time.

The Atkinson family moved into Bury House after the departure of Mr and Mrs Finch. By that time, they had two daughters, and four further daughters and a son were born between 1821 and 1825, during their turbulent time at Bury House.

Both national and local newspapers of 1825–26 described a suit for divorce brought by Elizabeth against her husband, 'by means of cruelty and adultery'. The report of the case determined in the Ecclesiastical Courts makes for interesting reading.

Thomas Atkinson was alleged to have had affairs with three local women, and from two of those relationships a child was subsequently born. The first liaison occurred shortly after the Atkinsons took up residency at Bury House and Elizabeth 'consented to forget and forgive' all of her husband's 'former infidelities if he would promise for the future to abandon his licentious habits'. However, further extra-marital relationships occurred from 1820 to 1824 while they were at Bury House.

A key witness in the case was a servant in the Atkinson household named Harriett Hobbs, described as 'a mere girl'. There arose the question of whether she had been bribed by Elizabeth's solicitor and under examination she confessed that her father received money 'for her use and in order to supply her with clothes [...] that her mother had actually purchased clothes for her with such money: and that Mrs Atkinson had furnished it'. Eventually the court found in favour of Elizabeth.

The Atkinsons both left Bury House during 1825. Thomas moved to Guernsey and then to Devon, where he died in 1875. Thomas Atkinson Junior continued to own Bury House until 1837. For part of the ensuing twelve years, the house remained empty, available for sale or lease. However, there was one notable resident during that period.

JOHN CLAVELL

From 1825–27, Bury House was leased to Captain John Clavell. He first went to sea in 1792 at the age of 13. In 1797 Clavell served under Flag Captain (later Admiral) Cuthbert Collingwood, Nelson's second in command at the Battle of Trafalgar. Collingwood became Clavell's mentor and as he moved from ship to ship he took Clavell with him, always as his first lieutenant.

In August 1805, Collingwood wrote to his wife, Sarah, '[…] this being for ever at sea wears me down; and if I did not have Clavell with me I should be ten times worse, for he is the person in whom my confidence is principally placed.'

Prior to the Battle of Trafalgar, they had transferred to HMS *Royal Sovereign*, which was to lead the British advance. The ship was severely disabled and five officers, twenty-nine seamen and thirteen marines were killed and ninety-four more were wounded, including John Clavell. Collingwood, now in command of the British fleet following the demise of Lord Nelson, had transferred his flag to HMS *Euryalus*, leaving Clavell in charge of *Royal Sovereign*.

In the aftermath of the battle, a severe storm occurred that caused more damage to the British fleet. *Royal Sovereign*, already reduced to a hulk, suffered badly. A great wave swept into the cabin and washed the wounded and unconscious Clavell from his cot and into the wardroom. Clavell would have drowned if Marine Captain Joseph Vallack had not grabbed his body and held on tight.

Having recovered from his injuries, Clavell assumed command of the sloop HMS *Weazle* and in 1808 was promoted captain and in command of HMS *Glatton*. Over the following seventeen years, he had various commissions, as well as periods on half-pay.

In April 1825, Clavell was appointed Captain of Portsmouth Ordinary, in charge of the unused vessels laid up in the harbour. Requiring a suitably sized local residence for his wife Charlotte, their five daughters and three sons, he moved to Bury House.

During the two years at Portsmouth there are records of him heading a government committee investigating the use of rockets to assist in ship-to-shore rescue in 1826. Then, on 18 February 1827, just before daybreak, one of the ships under his care, HMS *Diamond*, caught fire in the harbour. Despite the attempts by Clavell, together with the captain of HMS *Victory*, to get the fire under control, Diamond was destroyed. However, they succeeded in getting the ships nearest removed out of danger.

After leaving Bury House, Clavell held positions as Superintendent of the Dockyards at Falmouth and then Chatham and then in 1841 as Captain of Greenwich Hospital, where he died in 1846 at the age of 68.

THOMAS AND MARY SOUTH

Bury House was eventually sold in 1837 to Captain Philip Bridges RN, although records suggest that he and his wife, Harriet, were already living there by 1834. Their residency only lasted until 1840, when Bury House was purchased by Edward Tylee, a London solicitor. Clearly this was purely an investment opportunity, since there is no record of Tylee ever living in the property. Both the 1841 and 1851 censuses have Thomas South and his family as occupants of Bury House.

The story of Thomas South and the book written in Bury House by his eldest daughter Mary Anne is a bizarre one. The book has been described as 'one of the most curious in the annals of literature' and 'while never a bestseller, the book has enjoyed a certain positive notoriety'.

Thomas was an academic and Mary Anne collaborated with him from an early age. Although she received no formal education, she became proficient in Latin and Greek and developed an extensive knowledge of the classics. Thomas and Mary Anne shared a passionate interest in ancient religions and the study of Hermetism, a set of philosophical and religious beliefs including alchemy, astrology and ritual magic. He had a large library of rare books on religion and philosophy and his daughter helped him index the collection.

Their early studies led Thomas in 1846 to publish their first work, called *Early Magnetism*, then in 1849 they decided to prepare separate works based on their research into Hermetism. Thomas was to write an epic poem and Mary Anne a detailed reference book. They would work separately using the same research material and there would be no comparing notes and discussion until the projects were finished. By 1850, Mary Anne had completed her project – a book of over 500 pages, its short title being *A Suggestive Inquiry into the Hermetic Mystery*.

Thomas arranged to have the book published without first reading it. Privately financed by Thomas, it was published anonymously by Trelawney Saunders of London. Approximately 100 copies were sent out to libraries, reviewers and sold to purchasers. Finally, Thomas read the book, and he was horrified that it had revealed sacred secrets that alchemists had gone to great pains to hide through the clever use of cipher codes, puns and symbols. He wrote to the publisher forbidding sales of further copies, called in all unsold books at a cost of £250 and set about buying back as many copies as he could.

The books were brought from London to Bury House, where they were stacked upon the lawn. On top of the pile Thomas placed his own uncompleted manuscript 'The Enigma of Alchemy and Oedipus Resolved', which no one had seen, then with the apparent consent of Mary Anne they made a bonfire and burnt all copies.

Thomas South died at Bury House on 7 June 1858 and was buried at St Mary's Church, Alverstoke, seven days later. Mary Anne's work as an authoress came to an end and the family moved from Bury House shortly after Thomas's death.

In 1859, Mary Anne married Reverend Alban Atwood and moved to his parish in Leake, North Yorkshire. After Alban died, Mary Anne became reclusive but enjoyed corresponding with friends. She died at home on 13 April 1910 at the age of 91. Her last words were typically enigmatic, 'I cannot find my centre of gravity'. A copy of *A Suggestive Inquiry …* survived and was subsequently published in 1918. It has become a cult book.

The story of Mary Anne South lives on and has influenced thinking and cultural works down the years. Her papers, including 700 letters and manuscripts, were purchased by the John Hay Library at Brown University, Providence, Rhode Island, USA, in 1967.

HENRY DUNCAN PRESTON CUNNINGHAM

Henry Cunningham was born in Cornwall on 29 June 1814, the second son of naval surgeon Dr John Cunningham. At the age of 16 he followed his father into the Royal Navy and began an illustrious career. He gained an early distinction by single-handedly undertaking the dangerous task of surveying the carefully guarded defences of the Dardanelles and producing detailed drawings for the government.

In 1835, Cunningham moved to the civil line of the Royal Navy, initially as a captain's clerk, before qualifying for the rank of purser and later paymaster.

Although engaged in the civil line, Cunningham saw active service and was twice mentioned in dispatches for conspicuous gallantry, in China in 1842 and South Africa in 1845. In 1842, he became a key player during attempts to negotiate a peace treaty with Queen Ranavalona of Madagascar, for which he taught himself the local language.

In 1850 Cunningham married Frances Warden and they settled in Gosport the same year. Over the next four years, Frances gave birth to two sons and a daughter. In 1861, they purchased Bury House from Edward Tylee. It was a significant year in the life of Cunningham as he also left the naval service in order to pursue other interests that were to bring him international recognition.

It was as an inventor of important nautical and military equipment that Cunningham was to become famous, and he was already working on his engineering ideas while pursuing his naval career. His numerous inventions included an eccentric paddle wheel, a lifeboat and lifeboat carriage, atmospheric gun carriages, chain traversing gear for working gun turrets, shot carriages, slings and racks, and easy methods of working heavy guns for coast defence batteries and on board naval ships.

However, Cunningham's most famous invention was the self-reefing topsail. Early in his naval career, he had witnessed a terrible accident that was by no means rare, when a young seaman lost his life falling from the topsail of the ship while helping to reduce sail by working aloft. Cunningham succeeded in devising a system of reefing topsails, by which the amount of sail spread could be diminished or increased from the deck of the ship, without a single man going aloft. This ingenious invention met with immediate and widespread recognition and was fitted to thousands of vessels of all nations, lessening the dangers to seamen in unfurling and furling topsails in bad weather.

In 1861 Cunningham acquired the Gosport Iron Foundry & Workshop at the Green, originally set up by Henry Cort, to provide him with the means to develop and manufacture the self-reefing topsail and his other military inventions.

Cunningham served the local community in a number of ways. He was appointed a Justice of the Peace for Hampshire in 1861 and by 1863 had become Gosport's senior magistrate. He was chairman of both the Gosport & Alverstoke Young Men's Christian Association and the Army & Navy Institute, which offered beds to destitute sailors, soldiers and marines as well as pensioners and civilians. He was a supporter of the Gosport Ragged School and assisted in providing lessons in the art of seamanship

Cunningham was also involved with the 6th Hants (Gosport) Rifles and the 3rd Hants (Dockyard) Artillery Volunteers, becoming captain of the unit in 1861. Then in 1870, he was appointed major of the 1st Administrative Brigade of the Hampshire Artillery Volunteers.

In 1863, Cunningham commissioned a local surveyor to draw up a plan of Bury House and its grounds. It provides a clear indication of how it had evolved over nearly a century and a half. To the right of the main house a single-storey drawing room had been added. The brewhouse still remained but the other rear building, thought to be a laundry, had gone and was replaced with a small dairy and other ancillary units. The stables and coach house area had been modified and behind the house were extensive ornamental and kitchen gardens.

Henry Cunningham died suddenly at Bury House on 19 January 1875 at the age of 60. He was buried at Saint Mary the Virgin, Rowner. His unique headstone, carrying a carving of the self-reefing topsail, was moved from his original resting place when the church was extended and now sits on the green, landscaped area at the front of the church.

Shortly after Henry's death, Frances Cunningham left Bury House but continued to own it until 1893. She died in 1904 at her daughter's residence in Crescent Road, Alverstoke.

MARY HOWSE AND HER SON, REVEREND LAWRENCE CHAMBERLEN

Widow Mary Howse then took up residency on a five-year lease. She had moved from Cheltenham together with her son, Lawrence Chamberlen, and three daughters. Clearly the purpose of the relocation was to enable Lawrence, who had been ordained into the clergy in 1871, to take up a position at St Mary's Church, Alverstoke.

The appointment was to become controversial, in that Reverend Chamberlen was a member of an extreme religious group of clergymen known as the Society of the Holy Cross. An article in the *Hampshire Telegraph* of July 1877 named local members of the group, including Chamberlen, and the following edition carried an unsigned letter to the editor, headed 'The Cure For Confessors', naming four members of the society residing in the district, including Lawrence, who were claimed to be in approval of 'the disgusting manual called "The Priest in Absolution" surely the filthiest professional work ever printed'!

The controversy continued for several months before the *Hampshire Telegraph* of 10 October printed in full a letter that Lawrence had written to Canon Walpole, Rector of St Mary's, withdrawing from the society.

The letter stated that its intention had been as a private society for the promotion of holiness of life among the clergy. However, 'it has involuntarily become the subject to a publicity which its members never contemplated'. The letter carried a postscript:

> As my connection with the Society of the Holy Cross has naturally been the cause of some uneasiness among the members of those congregations in Alverstoke whom, under your direction I am privileged to minister, I shall be glad that the above letter may be made as public as you may judge to be necessary.

In 1879, Chamberlen was appointed vicar of Chatburn, near Clitheroe. However, Mary Howse continued to live in Bury House during the 1880s. By 1891 she was living at Lynwood House in Bury Road, where she died in February 1894. She was buried at Ann's Hill Cemetery.

BENJAMIN MARLOW

By 1891, the occupants of Bury House were Benjamin William Marlow, aged 71, a retired Inspector General of Hospitals A.M.D, his wife, Jane (57), daughter, Mary Elizabeth (28) and niece, Rosa S. Plummer (33). Marlow was born in Ireland in 1820 but clearly had family links to Gosport. He qualified as a surgeon in Edinburgh in 1842, then joined the army as an assistant surgeon, serving with the 28th (North Gloucester) Regiment of Foot. He was to remain with the regiment until 1865.

Marlow served during the Crimean War and was present at the Battles of Alma and Inkerman, as well as the Siege of Sevastopol. In May 1857, he received the Legion of Honour for his distinguished service in the war with Russia.

In 1862, he became surgeon major of the regiment, then in 1867, Deputy Inspector General of Hospitals. He retired in 1870 with the rank of Inspector General of Hospitals, Army Medical Department.

The Marlow family were based in Gosport for a number of years following his retirement. By 1891, they were living in Bury House, but they moved when Frances Cunningham sold the property in June 1893.

Benjamin Marlow died on 7 November 1894 and was buried in the family vault at St Mary's, Alverstoke, alongside Admiral Benjamin Marlow, who died in 1795, and General Marlow, who died in 1861. Jane Marlow died in 1915 and is also buried in the vault.

PETER AND EDITH HORDEN

On 7 June 1893, Frances Cunningham sold Bury House to Peter Hordern and his wife, Edith, for the sum of £1,600. Hordern was a retired civil servant, having been a senior superintendent in the education department in India and Director of Public Instruction in Burma from 1867 to 1888.

Their period of residency must have been the liveliest in the history of Bury House, since they arrived with seven children, aged between 2 and 13 years. They included Archibald (born 1889), who would later become Sir Archibald Frederick Hordern, Chief Constable of East Riding, Yorkshire, then later Cheshire and Lancashire.

It was evident that Peter Hordern had immediate plans to extend Bury House, because the month he acquired the property he submitted a planning application to the urban district council for additions it. This was followed by applications for a scullery and addition to the coachman's residence. The accommodation to the rear of the original house was added at that time, including the present main access.

Peter Hordern's time at Bury House was marked by a number of disputes with the urban district council. The first involved the discovery in 1893 by the council surveyor that part of the stables were being converted into a coachman's residence without planning permission. Then, in 1896, there was a dispute regarding the position of the front wall, and in 1905 Hordern complained that a passing place for tramcars opposite Bury House was shown on plans, contrary to his agreement with the council.

Peter Hordern died in 1913 and was buried in St Mark's Cemetery, Alverstoke. Edith continued to own Bury House until 1926. She died five years later and was laid to rest alongside her husband.

JOHN PARDOE

The next purchaser was John George Pardoe, a recently retired urological surgeon, and his wife. He made his career at the West London Hospital, where he was ultimately consulting surgeon. He was secretary of the Second International Congress of Urology in 1924 and of the Section of Urology in the last general International Medical Congress in London in 1913. John Pardoe continued to own Bury House until 1937, but by 1934, he and his wife had moved away and the property was let for the next two years.

REAR ADMIRAL CECIL TALBOT

The new occupiers were Rear Admiral Cecil Ponsonby Talbot and his wife, Bridget. His move to Gosport arose upon having been appointed Flag Officer Submarines at Fort Blockhouse.

Talbot had an illustrious naval career. He was born in 1884 in Bangalore, India, and at the age of 13 he joined the Royal Navy as a cadet, on board HMS *Britannia*, a wooden battleship moored in the River Dart. In 1900, he passed out top of his year, winning the Chief Captain's Prize. The following year, he joined his first ship, HMS *Glory*, on the China Station during the Boxer Rebellions. He was presented with an engraved officer's sword and later the Royal Humane Society's bronze medal for saving the life of a sailor who had fallen into the fast flowing Yangtze River.

In 1904, he joined the newly formed Submarine Branch, serving in the primitive and dangerous early submarines, which ran on petrol and batteries, both of which produce noxious gases. From service below the waves, his next venture took him above them as he became the first naval officer to attend an army balloon course.

In 1911, he was first lieutenant of HM Airship *No. 1*, an experimental rigid airship intended for observation at sea. Unfortunately, the airship broke up on its first flight and the crew and designers in the two gondolas had to swim for it. Talbot was formally commended for his role in preventing any casualties.

During the First World War, he served on submarines and then he worked his way up through the ranks until, in 1932, he was promoted rear admiral, the youngest admiral since Horatio Nelson.

When the lease on Bury House came to an end in January 1937, Cecil and Bridget moved to Woking, and he became Director of Dockyards at the Admiralty, a role he continued throughout the Second World War.

In 1939, Cecil was invested Knight Commander of the Order of the British Empire and, in 1947, Knight Commander of the Order of the Bath. In 1954, they retired to Cornwall, where Sir Cecil Talbot died on 17 March 1970.

STANLEY HUNT AND THE SECOND WORLD WAR

Bury House was sold by auction at the Swiss Café in Gosport High Street. The brochure announced the sale of the house 'with six roomed cottage and outbuildings in all nearly two acres' and gives a full description of the property at that time, including several photographs of the house and garden.

It concludes. 'The Residence is at present let to Admiral C.P. Talbot, C.B., D.S.O, at the rental of £160 yearly (tenant paying rates) but vacant possession will be given on 17 January 1937', then ominously, 'This sale affords an ideal opportunity to those wishing to acquire a residence of character. It should also be of particular interest to the speculative builder who desires a small estate for immediate development.'

The purchaser was local builder Stanley Hunt and his wife, Elfreda, so his intention for the use of his purchase was apparent from the outset. However, the Second World War intervened, so any plans for redevelopment of the site were put on hold.

During the war, Bury House was used as a hostel for families who had been bombed out of their homes and accommodation was also found for the headquarters of Rear Admiral R.S. McFarlan, commanding officer of the 32nd (Connaught) Battalion Home Guard. Formed in February 1943, it comprised the six dockyard home guard units on the Gosport side of Portsmouth Harbour, including Fleetlands, Priddy's Hard, Royal Clarence Yard and HMS *Daedalus*. In July 1945, Rear Admiral McFarlan, from his office in Bury House, wrote his reflections on the success or otherwise of the unit:

> The [Home Guard] Organisation administered by the War Office became – to some extent – an imposition upon Admiralty Establishments which they did not accept gladly … Had invasion come, the H.G. might have been better appreciated; as invasion did not come the H.G. were more or less of a nuisance.

GOSPORT MEMORIAL HOSPITAL

With the end of the war, Stanley Hunt was keen to revisit his plans to sell Bury House to a speculative builder who intended to demolish the property and put in a cul-de-sac for a new housing scheme. Enter Frank Chandler who, at the time, was Hunt's site foreman.

Throughout Frank's long life of 104 years, he had several connections with Bury House. During the 1970s he was interviewed by the Solent Tape & Audio Club, based at the GCA, and a copy of the cassette tape of his memoires is kept at the Hampshire Records Office in Winchester. From 1923 to 1958, Frank was on the management committee of the Gosport War Memorial Hospital, adjacent to Bury House, and fortune would have it that by 1945, he was the chairman. He could see a potential alternative use for the site that would include the retention of the historic house.

Together with colleagues, he persuaded Stanley Hunt to sell Bury House to the hospital for use as a nurses' hostel. In his taped memoirs, Frank comments that Stanley Hunt had agreed to the sale of Bury House to the War Memorial Hospital Trustees for £3,300, the same price as he paid for it eight years earlier. He concluded that, had they not taken this step, 'then Dr White would not have had Bury House as a community centre'.

At about the same time, the War Memorial Hospital Trustees bought Redclyffe Annex in The Avenue, Gosport, and decided it didn't need both properties. Consequently, Bury House remained unused from 1945–57 and fell into a state of disrepair. Eventually, on 27 Match 1957, it was sold by the Minister of Health for £2,500 to the Trustees of the GCA, of which Dr Leonard F.W. White, the Gosport Divisional Education Officer was chairman.

GOSPORT COMMUNITY ASSOCIATION (GCA)

The GCA was formed in 1947 by a group of enthusiastic members and met at Privett Secondary School, although from the outset its firm aim was 'to have a Centre which would reflect the cultured personality of the Borough' and which would provide surroundings in which members could spend their free time in a variety of pursuits.

The interest of the GCA in acquiring Bury House had commenced by May 1955 as a planning application was submitted to the council for alterations and additions to the property. In September 1958, with Bury House now in its ownership, the GCA submitted its first proposals for a dance hall and theatre adjoining the property. The project to provide the facilities and furnishings required a further £2,500. Of the total budget of £5,000, the Ministry of Education gave a grant of £1,000 and the remainder was raised by voluntary efforts.

In 1960, the Thorngate Ballroom, theatre and a suite of rooms were opened, the inaugural event being a dance with Victor Silvester and his orchestra.

During the GCA ownership, alterations have been made to Bury House. Initially, a new canteen was built to the right of the main building, its appearance designed to mirror the original drawing room on the left-hand side. The stable block was demolished to provide rear access to the centre and the brewhouse made way for the ballroom block, with the theatre behind Bury House and separated from it by a courtyard. In 1965, a stage and band room were built in the ballroom and the Agnew Room was added next to the ballroom. Then, in 1976, the single-storey extension to the left of the original house was replaced with a two-storey building of similar design. On 20 April 1983, Bury House achieved a Grade II listing.

CONCLUSION

My work in researching the history of Bury House arose from concerns that this historic property, one of the most striking Georgian buildings in Gosport, needed vital restoration work. The GCA Heritage Project was set up to seek significant grant funding for this work. Little was known about the history of the house and those who had lived in it, and it was considered that the prospects of securing funding would be greatly enhanced if it was discovered that there were previous occupiers of local or even national importance. To the best of my knowledge, the overarching financial aim of the project is yet to be achieved, but it is hoped that the documentation by The Gosport Society of the 300-year history of one of Gosport's most important buildings will provide a reference resource that can be used in future towards this objective.

5

BATTERY NO. 2 AND THE DIVING MUSEUM

Kevin Casey

No. 2 Battery, a Grade-II-listed building, is on Historic England's 'Heritage at Risk Register' and is one of the projects included in the five-year (2019–24) HAZ programme awarded to Gosport by Historic England. The battery was part of the coastal defence fortifications known as the Stokes Bay Lines. These were extensive fortifications, defensive moats, casemated earthworks and artillery emplacements around Portsmouth Harbour to protect the Royal Navy Dockyard (now HM Naval Base, Portsmouth).

In the nineteenth century, the Royal Navy Dockyard was considered the most important naval establishment in the British Empire. The Lines were proposed in 1857, largely as a consequence of heightened Anglo–French tensions, and Stokes Bay was considered the beach most suited to landing invading troops.

Construction commenced in 1859 and was completed in 1861, and the Lines ran from the rear of the Browndown Batteries, in the west, to Fort Monkton in the east. They consisted of five gun batteries and a moat system. No. 2 Battery, being the largest of the five batteries, was completely encircled by the moat with access via a fixed bridge. In 1878, the Royal Engineers diverted the local River Alver into the moat and in 1891 they constructed a sluice to the sea, west of No. 2 Battery, which was used to regulate the water level of the moat.

The battery was first armed with seven 8in smooth-bore guns, three firing east and four firing west from the casemates, with two 64-pounder rifled muzzle-loading guns mounted on the top facing the sea. In 1886, the east- and west-firing guns were replaced with 7in, 82cwt rifle breech-loading guns, while the top-mounted guns were replaced by two 7in, 7-ton rifled muzzle-loading guns.

The palm trees welcome visitors to the internationally reputed Diving Museum. (LM)

The former artillery placement No. 2 Battery (housing the Diving Museum) was one of several such batteries of the Stokes Bay Lines, a series of defensive moats and ditches covering Gosport's seaward approaches. (LM)

In 1891, the two top gun emplacements were rebuilt to take two 7in, 7-ton rifled muzzle-loading guns on Moncrieff disappearing carriages. By 1899, all the 7in rifled breech-loading guns were removed and by 1902 replaced with machine guns. Also by 1901, the Moncrieff carriages were removed and two emplacements for 6in breech-loading Mk VII guns were added on top of the Moncrieff pits, which were filled in but left in place. The 6in breech-loading guns were struck off the approved armament in 1902 and all machine guns were withdrawn in 1907, leaving the battery obsolete and unarmed.

In 1932, GBC purchased the battery from the Home Office. In 1933, the GBC approved the use of the site as a caravan park and in 1939 they moved their records from the Town Hall into the battery for safe archive storage.

During the Second World War the site was requisitioned by the War Office and was retained after the war. In 1947, it was used by the Special Armament Development Establishment, also known colloquially as 'The Wheezers and Dodgers', based in nearby Fort Gomer.

In 1950, the 7th Royal Tank Regiment Amphibious Wing of the British Army used the battery and some of the land was released by the military. GBC agreed with the military that the demolition of No. 2 Battery and the removal of the earth and hardcore could be carried out after 1951. The military released it back to GBC in 1951, and in 1956 the moat around it was filled in. The channel carrying the Alver River along the western side of the battery was left intact and the sluice gate connecting the sea at the southern end is still serving that purpose today.

In the 1970s, the remaining sections of the moat system were finally filled in.

In 1982, GBC transformed the bunker into their nuclear control bunker (as part of the national Civil Defence organisation during the Cold War). At this time, a new tunnel opened between what is now the entrance in the east-facing section into the magazines underneath the sea-facing gun emplacements.

The process of transforming the battery into a nuclear bunker required the total sealing up of the building by removing and bricking up all windows and doorways. Two anti-nuclear blast doors were installed as well as two air-filtration systems.

In the end, due to a modest thaw in East–West political relations, the transformation to protected nuclear bunker status was not completed. Civil Defence arrangements in the UK were eventually 'stood down' and the building became unused.

In 1990, GBC decided to utilise the battery as a historical tourist attraction. On the east face, the centre gun port was turned into a door and the other two ports into windows. Air vents were installed in all bricked-up windows and the rear bricked-up doorway, exposing the building to the outside environment. At this stage, they realised the costs were too high and subsequently the work stopped. The battery was shut and left unused. Occasionally it was opened to the public for short exhibitions, such as the commemoration of the 50th anniversary of D-Day (6 June) in 1994.

The wartime vintage Air Raid Precaution bunker in The Avenue holds the archives of the Historical Diving Society. (LM)

Today, among local defence structures, No. 2 Battery is the only near-complete battery remaining. Only small parts remain of No. 1, a scheduled monument located behind No. 2 Battery. There are no remains of Batteries 3 and 4.

No. 5 Battery is Grade-II listed and is much smaller, with a section having been demolished for an access road. It is located in the disused section of the Royal Naval Physiological Laboratory (currently the Institute of Naval Medicine) on Fort Road – a site owned by Qinetiq. The facility has been closed for several years and a developer is currently drawing up plans for limited housing on the site.

In 2009 the Historical Diving Society, an all-volunteer registered charity, was in the process of looking for a building to house its collection of diving equipment. It approached GBC to see if it would be possible to occupy and use No. 2 Battery to display their collection in a Diving Museum. Following negotiations in 2010, the council awarded them a 'Tenancy at Will' lease agreement for No. 2 Battery.

Due to the battery being unused and exposed to the harsh coastal environment for thirty years, it was in a poor state when the Historical Diving Society first occupied it. They had a huge task in front of them to carry out works that would make it suitable to display the collection.

Well, the small band of dedicated volunteers did it! In 2011, the Diving Museum opened to the public. As the museum is operated by volunteers, it only has the resources to open at weekends and on public holidays from April until October. The council and residents were pleased to see the building given a new lease of life and purpose after being closed for so many years. During the first year of opening, many local residents visited, just to look inside a building that they had grown up with, walked and driven past, but never had an opportunity to visit.

HISTORICAL DIVING SOCIETY OCCUPANCY –
SEEKING DEVELOPMENT FUNDING

The Historical Diving Society signed a ninety-nine-year lease for No. 2 Battery in 2021, but this came with a significant caveat – responsibility for the fabric of the building. At the moment, only a third of the battery space is usable as a museum. The physical conditions of the remainder of the building are not suitable for the general public or the display of exhibits. The long-term aim is to fully restore No. 2 and develop the museum into an important national and international standard exhibition space, displaying and recording the history of diving as well as highlighting the history of No. 2 Battery, the Stokes Bay Lines and the importance of Stokes Bay within the context of the defence of the realm.

The desire is to make both No. 2 Battery and the Diving Museum an asset for Gosport by saving one of its many historic buildings, telling one of Gosport's many stories, creating jobs and helping the local economy. To achieve these aims, the Historical Diving Society is working hard, applying for financial assistance in the form of grants. Two grant applications were submitted to Arts Council England in November–December 2021.

The first application was to the Museum Estate and Development Fund. If awarded, No. 2 Battery will become an exemplar project under this scheme. The lower passage temperature needs to be raised and equalised with the rest of the building and this will be achieved by laying an underfloor heating system on top of the existing floor, which will be reversible if required. The heating will be supplied by an air-source heat pump. Unusually perhaps, heating in summer is required as the heating differential from the lower section of the building is greater at that time of the year. During summer, the air-source heat pump will supply four units of heat for every unit of electricity. The temperatures will be monitored for the following

Fort Blockhouse, now surplus to military requirements, has long claimed to be the foundation home of the Royal Navy Submarine Service and naval diving. The famous water-filled submarine escape tower, destined for an alternative future under HAZ plans, rises above HMS Alliance, *the star international tourist attraction at the Royal Navy Submarine Museum. (LM)*

twelve months. According to our experts, heating a Victorian fortification using this method has never been attempted before.

The second grant application is to the Capital Investment Programme, which will deliver a disabled ramp to the front door and a platform lift inside, repair the gun emplacements and reinstate the rear door.

To complete the repairs to No. 2 Battery and develop the Diving Museum, grant applications were also to be made to the National Lottery Heritage Fund and Historic England in February 2022. If the applications are successful, the aim is for the museum to be open more days of the week and more weeks of the year. Staff will be employed, and youth training schemes introduced.

THE UNIQUE CHARACTER OF THE HISTORICAL DIVING SOCIETY

The Historical Diving Society was formed in 1990 by a group of diving enthusiasts with the aim of preserving the rich diving history of the United Kingdom. It was the first such society in the world. Today, there are fourteen other societies modelled on it, located around the globe from Europe to Russia to Australia and the Americas.

Why should the Historical Diving Society locate the Diving Museum in Gosport? Research by the society's founding chairman, John Bevan, discovered that Gosport can make a plausible claim to be the 'Home of Diving', thus making it the obvious UK location in which to establish the museum.

The inventors of the first practical diving helmet were brothers John and Charles Deane. In 1823, they patented a pipe-connected 'smoke helmet' to enable a firefighter to enter a smoke-filled room to save possessions and animals from burning buildings. Unfortunately, their invention was a failure as the fire brigade did not take up their invention. Undaunted, they came up with the idea that their invention could be adapted to enable men to venture down to shipwrecks to salvage lost cargoes. Their idea eventually led to the development of the first successful workable diving helmet in 1828.

John (1800–84) moved to Gosport, as it was the best location for gaining access to a large number of wrecks at a suitable depth around the Isle of Wight. John engaged the ship owner Henry Abbinett, who was owner of a public house called The Three Guns, in Beach Street, Gosport, to transport him and his equipment to the wreck locations.

Eventually Henry persuaded John to sell him a set of diving equipment. This made Henry the first person in the world to purchase a commercial diving set. The purchase may be regarded as the birth of commercial diving. This simple action quickly repeated itself around the world.

John Deane lived and worked in Gosport for ten years. His first wife, Agnes Norris (1800–44), is buried at Trinity Church in Gosport. A plaque has been laid on the location of her grave site.

Deane then moved to Whitstable, where he married his second wife, Sarah Ann Browning. He is buried in Ramsgate.

Perhaps the two most notable wrecks Deane dived on were the *Mary Rose* and the *Royal George.* No. 2 Battery is within sight of the two wreck locations in The Solent.

HMS *Royal George* was launched at Woolwich in 1756 and at that time was the largest warship in the world. It foundered off Spithead on 29 August 1782 as it prepared to lead a fleet to raise the siege of Gibraltar. The death toll of more than 800 lives remains today among the greatest losses of life at sea from a single shipwreck in British waters.

Due to the relatively shallow waters, the wreck became a shipping hazard and it needed to be moved. John Deane was engaged by the Admiralty to commence salvaging any items that could be removed from the wreck, blow up the remaining wreckage and level the site on the seabed. It was too big and complex a task for one man. Thus, Royal Engineers, led by Colonel Pasley, were trained by John Deane in his diving dress and work continued until the ship was destroyed.

The *Mary Rose* was discovered in The Solent when the tide exposed it enough for nets to get snagged on it. A fishing boat reported one such incident, and when Abbinett investigated, he found the net caught on a piece of wood protruding from the seabed, which he thought nothing of. Subsequently,

The Diving Museum interior exhibition floor and layout. (HDS)

John Deane investigated and found the net was snagged on a cannon. He realised he had found the Tudor flagship, *Mary Rose*. John dived periodically on the site between 1836 and 1840. The *Mary Rose* was then largely forgotten until its very public recovery in the late twentieth century.

Deane recovered artefacts from both wrecks such as cannon, cannon balls and wood. As there was nothing extrinsically valuable to salvage from the ships, a variety of items were recrafted from the wood to sell as souvenirs. These included miniature books, with the covers made from the wood, and snuff boxes. More substantial items made from salvaged materials are a long-case clock and a sword made from metal salvaged from the *Royal George* with the ship engraved on the blade.

MUSEUM STATUS AND EXHIBITION

The Diving Museum is fully accredited by Arts Council England, mentored by the National Motor Museum Beaulieu for exhibition status and is affiliated with the National Museum of the Royal Navy. A close working relationship is maintained with the Mary Rose Trust in HM Naval Base, Portsmouth. It is an active member of the South East Museums Development Programme and the Hampshire Military Museums Network.

The exhibits cover all areas of diving, including sport, military, commercial and scientific – and the contribution of Gosport in these thematic areas. There are three internationally significant exhibits on loan from the Science Museum in London.

One is the 1828 Deane helmet, which was converted from a smoke to a diving helmet. A second helmet – the James helmet of 1825 – is the oldest diving relic in the country and the second oldest in the world. It predates the Deane helmet, but it was not commercially successful. The third is the bust of Augustus Siebe, who started Siebe Gorman, arguably the best-known diving manufacturing company. All three exhibits are housed in two high-quality, environmentally controlled display cases.

There are three 1 x atmosphere suits, one being a German Neufeldt & Kuhnke, from around 1936; a Jim suit, which had been on display in the RN Submarine Museum and is now part of the permanent collection; and a Newt suit, donated by Subsea 7, which had been used in the North Sea oilfields. These suits were used to eliminate the possibility of the bends, the dangerous effects on a diver's bloodstream after exposure to extreme pressures during a deep-ocean dive. Such suits and decompression chambers were all part of the ever-evolving technology to make diving safer.

Also in the collection is a 1906 Halls-Rees helmet, developed for submarine escape. This model of helmet featured in two silent movies, *20,000 Leagues Under the Sea* (1916) and *Wet Gold* (1921). Recently, the latest submarine escape suit has been donated to the museum, so it will now be able to display the progress of the submarine escape process in the Royal Navy down the years. Vistors are able to contrast the new and the old in diving technology.

Three sets of important medals are also on display. Those of legendary RN frogman Lionel 'Buster' Crabb, OBE, GM (1928–presumed dead in 1956) are on loan from the National Museum of the Royal Navy. Crabb was awarded the George Medal during the Second World War for his work removing limpet mines from the hulls of ships in Gibraltar waters that were waiting to form part of Malta-bound convoys.

He gained notoriety as the diver (possibly on an MI6 mission) who disappeared when diving under a visiting Soviet cruiser in Portsmouth Harbour in 1956. Despite several published attempts to tell the tale, it remains a story cloaked in mystery as the records will not be released to the public for 100 years.

The second set of medals are those of William Bailey, who also served in Gibraltar. He received the George Medal for his work there and then received a second George Medal for activities with the 'P' parties, clearing the European ports from mines and munitions as they were liberated following D-Day.

The third set is from Syd Knowles, who dived with Crabb for many years.

A complete Jacques Cousteau scuba set, with the original box and which he presented to Lord Mountbatten, is also on display.

The evolution of the technology of the diving suit is apparent in these exhibits from the unique collections of the Historical Diving Society. (HDS)

The project of restoring No. 2 Battery and developing the Diving Muscum still has a long journey ahead, but the restoration process demonstrates the importance of thinking outside the box on how to repurpose a heritage asset, give it a new beginning and ensure the specialised history of diving lives on well into the future.

AN ADDITIONAL BUILDING – AIR RAID PRECAUTION (ARP) BUNKER, THE AVENUE, ALVERSTOKE

The Historical Diving Society has recently acquired a second building, a Grade-II-listed Air Raid Precaution (ARP) bunker dating from the Second World War. It is located adjacent to the local primary school in The Avenue, in Alverstoke.

In 1937, the Air Raid Precaution Act was passed by the UK Parliament just in case the prospect of war turned into reality. In the early years of the Second World War, between December 1940 and February 1941, the ARP bunker was constructed. It followed the standard Ministry of Works pattern of heavily concreted surface structure with steel blast doors on top of reinforced underground chambers.

In the latter part of 1940, the original ARP organisation morphed into the Civil Defence Corps and the bunker became the base of this organisation. Its functions included acting as a protected control centre for the fire brigade and the local group of ARP wardens during air raids.

ARP wardens had many tasks: fire watching, blackout protection, issuing of gas masks and distributing and helping to erect Anderson and Morrison bomb shelters, often in the gardens of residents in Gosport. Blackout drills, involving patrolling the streets to ensure the putting out of domestic lighting and the closure of curtains, have gone down in British wartime history – with a mixture of notoriety and respect!

As the Second World War progressed and the nightly Blitz continued, ARP wardens took on ever-more urgent work: first aid, searching rubble for casualties, organising rescue parties, putting out local fires from incendiary bombs until emergency services arrived and reporting all incidents and addresses to the control centre. The famous 'All Clear' sirens that eerily signalled the end of an air raid in towns and cities across the nation were often sounded on the basis of ARP information. The ARP worked closely with the police force, the Royal Observer Corps and the Women's Voluntary Service.

During the Second World War at least sixty-one air raids on Gosport by the Luftwaffe were reported, involving the dropping of some 411 high-explosive bombs and more than 10,000 incendiaries. Some 111 civilians and three Civil Defence wardens were reported killed and more than seventy seriously injured, 454 homes were destroyed and 933 were seriously damaged. A mass grave for wartime casualties is in Ann's Hill Cemetery, the site marked by a commemorative stone.

Since 1968, when the Civil Defence Corps ceased using The Avenue bunker, it was unused, except for a brief period when the Scout movement used it. The structural design of ARP bunkers is such that limitations on future civil use are considerable; Grade II listing compounds this. However, in October 2011, the Historical Diving Society approached Hampshire County Council (HCC) with the request to use the bunker to store their reference library and reserve collection. This was agreed.

In 2015 the Historical Diving Society took over the freehold of the bunker from HCC. Volunteers have since cleaned and repaired the building, arranged its interior for storage, cleared much of the tangle of vegetation that for years hid it from view of passers-by on The Avenue, and established a wildflower garden to the frontage so the public can now see this unusual and rare structure from wartime. The structure is believed to be the last survivor of its age and type in Hampshire.

6

A SYNOPSIS OF THE HISTORY OF GOSPORT MUSEUM AND GALLERY

Margaret Ventham

When the time came to repair the damage done to Gosport during the Second World War, there was a mood of optimism in the 1950s and later for rebuilding in the 'modern style'. Redevelopment of the town and sites used for defence began to gather pace. Manufacturing processes and services were becoming automated. Local people talked about the changes to places where they used to work, walk, shop and spend their spare time. They began to save artefacts, documents, maps, pictures and photographs to recall the Gosport they remembered before it disappeared.

A group of enthusiasts got together to collect heritage material. Their purpose was to record the town's history for future generations. In 1970, this group founded the Gosport Historical Records and Museum Society. They used an old wooden shed in South Street for storing some of their collections – not ideal premises. In May 1972, the embryonic society exhibited their collections at the school hall in the old, art-nouveau-inspired brick building at the top of the High Street. These premises were the former County Grammar School and were occupied at that time by the Education Offices. The exhibition attracted nearly 3,000 visitors in five days!

GBC was as enthusiastic as the society and earmarked rooms, occupied at that time by the library, on the ground floor at the front of the old school for a museum using the society's collections. These rooms became available when the Library Service opened a new building in 1974. The Museum Society eventually morphed into The Gosport Society* and was invited to move the collections. The council provided an archivist and the donated

---

* For additional detail on the origins of the Gosport Historical Records and Museum Society, see: Murray, Louis, *The Gosport Society 1970–2020: The First Fifty Years* (The Gosport Society in association with LDJ Educational, 2020).

The Gosport Museum and SEARCH Gallery is located in the Old Grammar School at the western end of Gosport High Street. Now under the direction of Hampshire Cultural Trust, major renovations are under way to create a cultural hub, museum and exhibition space. (GP)

collections were accessioned for display in the new Gosport Museum. With help from many volunteers, GBC ran the museum and the gallery in the school hall from 1975 and Denise Coutts became a curator.

In 1991, HCC took over the old building, including the museum and gallery. The Education Offices moved to Havant to cover a larger area. Ian Edelman was appointed museum curator. He suggested volunteers become Friends of Gosport Museum (FOGM) and join the British Association of Friends of Museums. This they duly did – Margaret Roberts was the first member of FOGM. Membership rose to over 100.

The Friends stewarded the museum displays, ran a coffee bar and raised funds for whatever was needed, including a computer, microfiche reader, OS maps and museum interpretation material. They socialised, went on excursions, published articles and used a room on the first-floor corridor as a base and research room. In the style of *Doctor Who*, a 'Time Space Machine' was invented for the museum. It showed the origins of the area from early times up to the Ice Age – the video tape still exists. It was popular and remembered by visitors, who ask what happened to it!

SEARCH, a hands-on activity centre for the educational museum, opened in 1995 in the space vacated by the Education Offices, and a lift was added. The original team working there were Isobel Hughes (manager and history officer) and Ann Nicol (science officer). The support staff included

The Old Grammar School has been a functioning landmark in Gosport for more than 100 years. The blue plaque records some of its colourful history. (LM)

an administrator, caretaker and casual workshop leaders, including Janet Wildman, and later, Wendy Redman, who both became managers.

SEARCH utilised and made accessible the large number of generic social history objects that had been donated to Gosport Museum in the 1970s and 1980s. These objects, given by so many local people, were not specifically related to Gosport and could not tell the story of the town itself, but they wonderfully supported the curriculum of local schools. Because there is no public access to that part of the building, visiting school children were able to move freely around the room sets and activities when they visited SEARCH. The educational activities provided by the staff were designed to match the ages of the visitors. SEARCH has been and continues to be an outstanding success.

David Kemp was an avid collector of local geology samples and fossils. He had explored the local shores since boyhood. When he was working at the museum, he set up the Geology Gallery as part of the museum. He provided material he had found and identified. The gallery was dedicated to his memory. SEARCH will continue to use his collections in future.

In more recent years, what might be called the 'digital age' was developing. Footfall into traditional museums was beginning to drop. Nomenclature for public libraries began to change. The concept of 'Discovery Centres' came into vogue. HCC decided to combine Gosport Central Library with Gosport Museum as a pilot for such a centre.

The plan was put into operation in 2004. A new style of self-guided museum would be created on the mezzanine floor of the library. The museum in the Old Grammar School was dismantled. The collections were stored upstairs. Textile artefacts went to HQ to be better conserved. The original museum research room became a work space for SEARCH. The Geology Gallery, however, stayed in situ. The emptied museum rooms in the old building became a facility for local and family studies.

Work to create Gosport Discovery Centre took a year to complete and it opened to considerable public interest in 2005. The redesignation and repurposing was indicative of a wider-world trend towards public provision of such centres.

The Museum-on-the-Mezzanine was a storyboard presentation showing nearly 300 years of local and social history. Also provided were cabinets and drawers of artefacts from the earlier museum. Activities for youngsters and adults included two touch-screen computers – one with vintage photos of the area and the other with a program called 'Fortress Gosport'. The latter was a pictorial historic tour of the town defences from Roman through to late-Victorian times. Rearranging guns, rampart military impedimenta, etc. on a touch screen was highly motivating to children. Sadly, both screens eventually stopped working and the programs were not saveable.

The Discovery Centre is the modern name for the Central Public Library. As part of HCC Library Service, it stands opposite the Old Grammar School and complements that building through its comprehensive local studies collection of print and visual material resources about Gosport. (GP)

Similarly, local photographs had been photocopied and made available in album files for people to browse. Copies could be bought and those files have survived.

Before the original museum went into storage mode, the FOGM were advised that their help would no longer be needed! Newer work imperatives were viewed as 'technical/professional'. Franchise arrangements entered the picture and, among other functions, resulted in a commercial café in the Discovery Centre. The new museum facility would not need stewarding.

The membership of the FOGM consequently fell drastically. In 2008, Janet Wildman was managing SEARCH, the gallery and the new museum facility. History repeated itself. She invited the Friends to volunteer yet again! The staff needed help in the museum stores and at the mezzanine for events such as the HM Queen Elizabeth's Diamond Jubilee and the 2012 Olympics.

FOGM membership picked up somewhat, but in 2010 another major change was on the way. The Renaissance Fund for the Arts was ended. Hampshire lost £1 million of annual government support. The Arts Council was renamed Arts Council England. County and municipal councils now had to apply for grant-aided support from that and similar sources to keep functioning.

Financial cuts to local authorities took effect in 2011 and staffing was reduced by a third. More cuts were forecast. Charitable trusts have access to grants, gift-aided donations and merchandising opportunities. HCC decided to protect its museums, galleries and arts centres by operating these venues through a charitable trust but one registered as a business. Dr Janet Owen, director of the County Museum Services, began the task of creating a suitable trust.

Meanwhile, in 2012, the costings associated with the Old Grammar School building were integrated into the library budget. (This budget transfer would assist the financial start-up of the trust.) The Discovery Centre gained more space for fiction and the children's library by transferring the Hampshire Naval Collection and other material to the SEARCH workroom.

The museum research room was boxed up and stored, providing some extra storage space for SEARCH, and stored geology material went to the Hampshire Cultural Trust premises at Chilcomb, near Winchester. This resulted in the freeing of two rooms for hiring and two offices were emptied and repurposed for letting to suitable organisations, with filing cabinets moved into the museum store. A grant was obtained to redecorate the old building.

One of a kind? The 'Creative Seagull With Attitude' certainly is. Hampshire Cultural Trust maintains a pop-up museum and gallery information base on the High Street while the Old Grammar School undergoes renovation. (LM)

Museum volunteering changed from weekly to monthly. Income from hiring rooms and offering courses helped, but Hampshire Museum and Library Services lost more staff before Dr Owen achieved the foundation of the Hampshire Cultural Trust on 1 November 2014.

The Hampshire Cultural Trust has successfully moved on to operate certain HCC museum and cultural facilities, despite some restructuring due to further austerity measures. By 2016–17 the HCC Library Service was no longer able to carry the budget for the Old Grammar School building. The Mus-on-the-Mezz was reduced to a display using the original cabinets, but the storyboards and activities disappeared. Local and Naval Studies returned once more to the Discovery Centre.

In April 2018 the Old Grammar School building finally became the responsibility of Hampshire Cultural Trust. The trust decided to have a venue manager and a visitor service assistant at each of its sites and a schools manager for SEARCH in Gosport. Staff were appointed and plans put in place to repurpose and develop the old building. A new museum would be created, along with facilities for generating income from a café and shop. SEARCH would focus on natural sciences on the upper floor and ground-floor rooms would be prepared for public use.

Still Life – Static displays of memorabilia and Gosporteers from different eras often feature in the exhibition spaces of the Discovery Centre and the Gosport Museum and Gallery. (LM)

Grant funding for the redevelopment was being planned when town centres, affected by online shopping and store closures, became a national problem. The government asked Historic England to choose suitable sites for high street regeneration by funding the HAZ scheme. Municipal councils were able to apply for financial assistance under this and similar schemes.

A successful application for funds was put together by GBC, Hampshire Cultural Trust and The Gosport Society. Gosport was chosen because the former Old Grammar School is a Grade-II-listed, heritage building in a High Street needing regeneration. The old school building will be repurposed for the twenty-first century as a cultural and public education hub. It will be renamed Gosport Museum and Art Gallery. With the support of local people and their treasured memories, the new manifestation of the museum will open. The FOGM were pleased to receive a £50,000 bequest from Margaret Roberts to be used in her memory for the new museum. The long story of an important local institution continues!

7

MARTIN SNAPE (1852–1930): CELEBRATED GOSPORT LANDSCAPE ARTIST

Richard Martin

Martin Snape, Gosport's celebrated artist, died ninety-two years ago between the two world wars, but his contribution to the topographical history of his hometown through much of the Victorian period and into the early twentieth century remains unparalleled.

Martin was born at Spring Garden Cottage, just a stone's throw outside of the historic town ramparts, on 31 December 1852. He was the first of six children born to Alfred and Sarah Snape, who are each listed in the 1851 census as 'painter and teacher of drawing'. One of his brothers, William, born ten years later in 1862, was an artist of equal ability and merits a separate article. His life was cut short in tragic circumstances in 1904, aged just 42 years.

An extract from a mid-Victorian guide to the town of Gosport states:

Being in the immediate vicinity of the great naval rendezvous of the kingdom, of which it may be said to form a part, and possessing within itself considerable advantages for shipping, Gosport has become a town of much importance, especially in time of war. Numerous public works have been established for supplying the wants of the navy, and extensive barracks for the military. At Priddy's Hard, northward of the town, are immense magazines of gunpowder, etc, for the supply of the army and navy. In the town there is a great iron foundry, for the manufacture of anchors and other articles for shipping.

The Richard Martin Gallery on Stoke Road.

An evocative Snape painting of Gosport waterfront. (Courtesy RM)

Most of Gosport's population at this time (less than 20,000) lived within the old ramparts, designed to protect the town and harbour from landward attack, the construction of which began in the seventeenth century. The historic old town bustled with life and would certainly have been very over-crowded. In 1851, there were 104 courtyards and alleyways recorded.

An event of significant importance to Gosport was the opening of the railway station on 29 November 1841. It would serve the residents of the town until 1953, and freight traffic until 1969. The grand station, designed in the Italianate style by Sir William Tite, was described by a historian in the 1970s as 'one of the finest pieces of station architecture surviving from the beginning of the railway age'.

It was just nine years after the opening of the Gosport railway line that Martin's parents moved to Spring Garden Cottage, a handsome double-bay-windowed Georgian building just two doors along from the station. In years to come, the railway line would open up the Hampshire countryside for Martin, who would often set off along the Meon Valley line with his easel and brushes.

Part of the station still exists. After being neglected and derelict for decades, the remains of the structure were rebuilt and modified to incorporate offices and housing. The result is an award-winning modern residential complex that retains the look of the original station. Perversely, and as Gosport residents are fond of reminding anyone who will listen, the town is one of the largest in the country without a railway station.

Martin Snape was educated at Burney's Academy, housed within a fine Georgian building a short walk away from the family home. Founded in 1791 by Dr William Burney, the academy was situated near the water's edge in Clarence Square. An early prospectus states:

> The establishment is of large extent and eligibly situated in a fine open square, opposite the dockyard and adjoining Portsmouth Harbour. Its situation offers many advantages to military as well as to naval pupils. At the Academy, delightfully situated in Coldharbour, Gosport, a limited number of young gentlemen are genteelly boarded, tenderly treated and instructed in every branch of useful and polite literature.

TENDERLY TREATED?

Local historian H.T. Rogers wrote of Martin Snape in his article for The Gosport Society publication, *Gosport Records* (No. 4, May 1972, pp. 16–20):

> His father was quite well-to-do, and all his sons were sent to Burney's Naval Academy in Clarence Square where the fees were fifty-two guineas a year, which was a lot of money in those days. Later, Alfred Snape was heard to complain that the money had been wasted. Certainly, it was a queer kind of training for young Martin. Parents who wanted their boys to become Naval officers and pass the stiff examinations would send them to a 'crammer' whose job it was to beat the required knowledge into their heads. Burney's was designed for this one purpose and had a high percentage of success,

but it is to be doubted if the methods employed provided much artistic grounding or would be approved today.

Nonetheless, Martin would become an erudite man, largely through his own studies. He would often take the train to Winchester, where he would spend hours in the records department gleaning as much knowledge as he could on Britain's history, topography and ancient buildings, particularly those of his native Hampshire. He had an insatiable appetite for learning and even developed an impressive grasp of Latin, regularly using Latin quotations in his letters and writings.

Edward Prideaux-Brune, the greatly loved rector of Rowner Church from 1884 to 1919, had similar interests and inevitably the two were to meet and form a lifelong friendship, during which time they exchanged hundreds of letters. Thankfully, many of Snape's letters to Prideaux-Brune exist in public and private collections and, apart from the numerous references to literary and ecclesiastical topics, contain much on such diverse subjects as the derivation of local place names, field names, the beauty of oak woods at Rowner, folklore, natural history, the politics of the day, voluminous notes on Nicolas Tindal (1687–1774), one-time Rector of Alverstoke, the ever-changing Portsmouth Harbour and many references to buildings, churches and landmarks around Gosport, its environs and elsewhere.

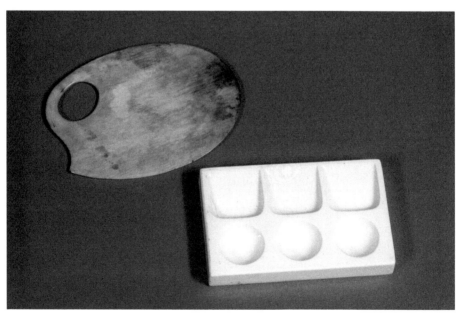

In the private collection of the Richard Martin Gallery is the unusual bone palette and paint-mixing dish that were used by Martin Snape. (Courtesy RM)

LANDSCAPE CORRESPONDENCE AND A DEVELOPING SENSE OF PLACE

One such letter, headed 'Spring Garden Cottage, 18th February1893', includes the following passage:

> How much we should like to know more about those men who saw the same sun and sea that we see, and cared more for the earliest buds and flowers of Spring than we do, and to whom each plant had its history and uses, while to us they are merely weeds, or connected with strange theories of evolution, and may be gathered whether under the dominium of Saturn, or influenced by the unruly actions and passions of Mars & Venus. If ever you think of any local names for plants, I wish you would make a note of them for my benefit. There are few more interesting things connected with our language than plant names.

Another, dated 1 October 1893, clearly indicates what a different proposition was a trip from the Snape family home at Spring Garden Cottage to St Mary the Virgin Church at Rowner, just under 2 miles to the north, in the pre-motorised days of the late-Victorian era, 'The weather was so bad this morning that I did not get further on the road to Rowner than Northlands, with a long intermediate halt at Willies abode [his artist brother's home at Camden Street, Forton]'.

The Snape take on Stoke Lake, a pleasant town backwater and a favourite subject for artists of contrasting styles. (Courtesy RM)

Edward Prideaux-Brune was held in extremely high esteem by Martin, who commenced every letter 'Reverend and Dear Sir' and would often sign off deferentially 'yours obediently'.

ROWNER CONNECTIONS

The Prideaux–Brunes were a wealthy, land-owning family dating back to the Norman Conquest. Such was the close friendship and mutual respect between Edward and Martin it seems likely that the former sponsored many of Martin's painting trips to other parts of Britain and occasionally Europe.

The manor of Rowner was granted to the Brune family in 1277 and subsequently the Prideaux-Brunes from 1799. The original Church of St Mary the Virgin, mentioned in the Domesday Book, retains the family chapel of the Prideaux-Brunes. It has served the community for nearly 1,000 years. It still stands in the vestiges of Rowner Copse, despite fires requiring its partial rebuilding, and area bombing in the Second World War. In the early twentieth century, the population of Rowner was just 374, which included the 240 occupants of Fort Grange, leaving just 134 residents of the parish.

Martin's close association with Rowner and its rector, in addition to his great interest in fieldcraft, were to influence his early paintings, which were almost exclusively of natural history subjects from the locality. Superbly executed, some were accepted by the Royal Academy for their prestigious exhibitions. Two such exhibits were 'The Gamekeeper's Museum' of 1883 and 'The Ferret Hutch' of 1894. Sadly, however, pictures of birds and animals did not sell well and for several years Martin would augment his meagre income by giving occasional art lessons, both privately and at various schools around the town.

COMMERCIAL ARTISTRY

Towards the end of the nineteenth century, and keen to become more commercial, Martin started to paint views in and around Gosport, Portsmouth Harbour, the Hampshire countryside and sometimes further afield. The public responded to this change of direction and Martin was to spend the first two decades of the twentieth century in relative comfort, working daily, often on commissions, from the first-floor studio at the Snape family home at Spring Garden Cottage.

Snape's mother, Sarah, died in 1899 and his father in 1911. Martin married Lydia, the widow of a naval officer, in 1899, and they would continue to live in the cottage for the rest of their lives. Snape's view south-east from his studio window took in the newly built St George Barracks, in one direction, and the Royal Clarence Victualling Yard in the other, the two establishments flanking the town gate through the ramparts spanning Forton Road. Here, he successfully painted countless views of the ever-changing town and its buildings until the lean years of the 1920s.

The inevitable drop-off in picture sales led him to live in rather difficult circumstances until the end of his life. He once again needed to supplement his income by giving private art tuition. A letter sent to me in 1991 from an elderly gentleman living in Portchester recalled Martin giving him tuition in the 1920s, 'He was a quiet, kind, inward-thinking man who dressed badly and needed a shave most times.'

His paintings, in both watercolour and oils, have great charm as well as accuracy, and his friend Frederick Davidson, a former art master at Gosport Secondary School, who drew the only known portrait of Martin in 1928, would later write:

> Martin Snape's recording of the ever-changing scene in and around Portsmouth Harbour from sunrise to sunset, at low and high water, the stench of the mud and vibrating greens, those rusty hulks against a background of yachts and the might of the navy, has never been so vividly portrayed by any other artist of the time.

Martin was equally happy using both watercolours and oils and enjoyed experimenting with different techniques. One of these was to use watercolour, heightened with plenty of body colour on tinted paper, giving a pleasant luminosity to the work.

His many views of Portsmouth Harbour, painted through the Edwardian period and into the 1920s, depict just about every type of vessel from the sailing era to dreadnoughts. More often than not, his harbour views would include HMS *Victory* afloat on the Gosport side, where the great ship was moored for over 100 years after her return from Trafalgar. Many views show the old ferry-landing stages and the adjacent shoreline sprinkled with wonderful old eighteenth- and nineteenth-century buildings.

Other views, within the town, depict ancient streets and premises, including Henry Cort's historic foundry at 18a The Green. A wall plaque currently marks the spot. This was one of the buildings lining this ancient area between what is now Mumby Road and the back of the High Street.

In this house on the corner of Spring Garden Lane and Forton Road, Martin Snape lived and worked, creating artworks of great visual merit, capturing the essence of Gosport and its environs. (LM.)

An annual fair was held here until 1901, when the council bought out the rights for £100 as they felt it lowered the tone of the town. Cort, known as 'the father of the iron trade', acquired his premises in 1776 and here discovered the process of converting pig iron into a soft, malleable condition. Snape described the building as 'possibly the oldest in town'.

Sadly, the infamous 'Gosport wrecking ball' of the mid-twentieth century demolished much of the historic old town and its environs. The much-changed appearance of the area now gives extra resonance to Martin Snape's paintings. They are a pictorial record of a built estate that has gone forever. One can only muse on what the artist's thoughts might be if he were able to gaze upon the area today!

PERSONAL INTEREST

A lifelong Gosportian, I founded my Stoke Road gallery business in 1980, a few hundred yards away from its present site. At that time, it was roughly equally divided between antiquarian books, antique prints and paintings. The emphasis was on items of local interest and, of course, Martin Snape figured prominently. Several of our older clients in those early days could remember meeting him and, indeed, as described above, some had received art lessons from him. One old gentleman gave me a bone mixing pallet, which Snape's widow Lydia had given him after her husband's death in 1930. I still treasure it!

Richard Martin Gallery has grown considerably over the past forty-two years and currently occupies a prominent site at Nos 19, 21 and 23 Stoke Road. My wife, Elaine, and two of my three sons, Daniel and Ben, work with me and are involved in most aspects of the fine art business, including picture restoration, framing and exhibitions.

Martin Snape and his work have always been of particular interest to us. I occasionally give lectures on him and his work to local groups and societies. We have examined, authenticated, restored, framed, valued, purchased and sold hundreds of his paintings and, although several decades have elapsed since his death, interest in the man and his work remains undiminished today. Fortunately, Martin was a prolific artist and many of his paintings survive in museums, local council offices and private collections to form a remarkable record of how the historic old town once looked.

He died on 24 November 1930 and his wife Lydia on 5 September 1933. They are buried together in the churchyard of St Mary the Virgin at Rowner, the parish he loved so well. A newspaper report of Martin's funeral stated:

> The funeral of Mr Martin Snape, the distinguished Gosport artist, took place yesterday at Rowner Churchyard, a fitting resting place for one who found much inspiration for his artistic work in the gentle scenery of this part of Hampshire. Although he shrank from publicity, he took a full part in the life of the community. He was vice-chairman of the library committee, a governor of the then technical school and a founder member of the Rotary Club of Gosport. The town's artistic and literary life has been made poorer by his passing.

Very few names from Gosport's distant past still have resonance today. That of Martin Snape is certainly one of them.

8

LEE-ON-THE-SOLENT: A 'NEW TOWN' DEVELOPMENT IN THE BOROUGH OF GOSPORT

Brian Mansbridge

THE SHAPING OF A NEW TOWN

Lee-on-the-Solent lies some 3 miles west of Gosport town centre but within the administrative boundaries of the borough. It is largely a seafront, residential settlement fronting The Solent and opposite the Isle of Wight. The *Cassini Old Series* map (1810–11) of the area shows a scattered, rural community of some four hamlets, Swag, Melvil, the prominent Court Barn and Lee.

The more modern settlement grew as a late-Victorian enterprise from Lee Farm, when the entrepreneur Sir John Robinson had a vision of developing a resort town from Solent farmland. This was a risky venture that was only viable as the project of a wealthy family. The project was reportedly paid for by his father, already a landowner in Swanage.

The initial plans were drawn up by Charles, son of John Robinson, in the early 1880s. The lack of any local development except tracks to farms gave Charles the freedom to design a new town on a grid layout. His broad streets, open spaces and a wide sea promenade gave a fine sea frontage for prestigious properties. Roads were laid out by the late 1880s and names taken from local farms: 'Lee', 'Milvil', and much later, 'Cherque', or from the manors of 'Britten' and 'Broom.' Added to this were names from the families' ancestral homes of Nottingham and Norwich, as well as from the Robinsons' adopted domicile of Swanage and the family home, 'Newton'.

Sir John was also the Surveyor of Pictures to Queen Victoria, which would explain the presence of patriotic names like 'Victoria' and 'Osborne'. Later, as the town expanded, names of prominent people in the early days of development were used, such as 'Clanwilliam', 'Petrie' and 'Raynes'. Unsurprisingly, the town's connecting roads were Gosport and Portsmouth Road and at the heart of the new resort, Marine Parade and Pier Street.

The layout and nature of this Victorian 'new town' was equally resolute. The layout would make the most of The Solent views, envisaged as a resort destination to compete with Southsea or Bournemouth. The building plots were a generous, regular shape and sold in forty-eight auctions between 1884 and 1901. The prestigious plots on the seafront had restricted covenants to prevent trade premises and the design had to be approved by the Robinsons' architect.

At the settlement centre was Victoria Square, earmarked for a church and open space. Mid-town plots, back from the seafront, were reserved for commercial properties bounded by the residential streets. There was a determination that this would not become a shabby town. Even these plots had covenants to build on a fixed line, set back behind front gardens and to a minimum spend per property. Back lanes or service roads just adequate for a horse and cart were laid out for tradesmen and rubbish collection – although today these same back lanes are awkwardly narrow for modern bin-collection vehicles and garage entrances.

Any difficulty in getting interested investors, in the early auctions, to this remote section of coastline was overcome by providing transport from Fareham together with a fine champagne lunch at the Victoria Inn, now the popular Bun Penny on Manor Way. Sales were to 'high society' and the absence of social or terraced housing is evidenced, as many houses were large enough to have sufficient servants' quarters included.

A factor that set the eclectic nature of building styles across the new town was that plots had to be fenced off within six months. However, no subsequent timescale was set for building works. This is in contrast to the way towns are normally developed. Unusually, plots were not sold expanding regularly from the centre but in various locations on the Robinsons' newly acquired land. This led to homes being built at various times to reflect the fashions and styles over a number of years.

A more significant factor to shape Lee was that the Robinsons also had to deal with the Delmé Estate, which owned parcels of farmland within the growing town. The Delmé family controlled most of the hinterland towards Fareham, leading to disputes over access roads. Delmé Estates took the advantage of pricing additional land sales as development land, not at farmland prices. This explains why some road names changed – the Lee Estate owned the High Street and Cambridge Road, but they were separated by a wedge-shaped Delmé field in the middle.

Gradually the Robinsons acquired more Delmé land and the High Street and Cambridge Road joined up in nature, if not in name. Public rights of way to Fareham were improved but also at an ever-increasing cost, a factor that encouraged the Lee Estate Office to purchase War Department land across Browndown military ranges. This land was purchased at more favourable rates, allowing the development of the Portsmouth Road and the opportunity of better connections with Gosport.

These acquisitions also allowed a railway connection by 1894, which was wholly appropriate for a growing resort. These new public links enabled locals not owning their own means of transport access to enjoy the seaside and the joys of a new pier, complete with entertainment and dances in the Assembly Rooms.

The Robinsons did recognise the need for some workers to support the resort. By the late 1880s, a few terraced houses and cottages were built – but well out of the centre, on land originally identified for stabling. This was one of the earliest changes to the original plan. The area for stables was released as the more affluent residents were among the early adopters of the motor car. Those without their own transport, particularly day trippers, could come by the faster and more comfortable train.

Brick workers' houses remain as the terrace on the Gosport Road, near the local primary school. Brickmaking was a necessary in-situ industry as the growing town required bricks, which were too heavy to transport far.

By the 1890s, land sales were picking up with 900 plots sold but still mostly to investors with predominantly big houses and mainly occupied in the summer. A census in the early 1890s revealed the winter population was only estimated to be about 250 souls.

It was in 1901, the year of Queen Victoria's death, that the Lee Improvements Committee was formed, the forerunner of the current Lee Residents Association. This committee became important in encouraging the parish council, then Crofton Council, and the district council to develop services such as sewage disposal and street lighting to meet the needs of a growing resort town.

By 1905, a council school was set up for the children of the town's workers. Until then, only private schools existed. Nonetheless, these were important in the early days of Lee. The Royal Naval Academy, later Trafalgar House School, brought professionals and academics who took an interest in the development of the town and these schools required the support of local services. The professional newcomers were also year-round residents, without servants to support their daily needs, nor a spare day to go to Fareham for supplies.

THE MILITARY ALSO SHAPES THE GROWING TOWN

The coastal Browndown military ranges had been used for firearms training even before the development of the town. Some 7,000 soldiers returning from the Crimean War were billeted on the ranges under canvas. The First World War saw another surge in use and so many locally billeted service-men that a certain Miss Kilburn donated part of her garden in South Place for a Catholic church – the forerunner of the current church of St John the Evangelist. So, the eastern part of Lee was expanding, but why did the west-ern end of Lee develop quite differently?

Victoria Square, with its tin church and fine view along Osborne Road, looking directly across The Solent to Queen Victoria's residence of Osborne House on the Isle of Wight, was clearly the original centre, with a square grid of streets around it. The difference in expansion to the east and west was all due to a 'temporary' requirement to increase seaplane training to counter the growing First World War submarine threat from the original but cramped facilities at nearby Calshot, across Southampton Water.

Westcliffe House, completed in 1904 and described as 'of exuberant Edwardian style', was was quite possibly a grand show house on the seafront. It had different facades to show fashionable styles and was complete with luxuriant interior detail. Whatever its envisaged future, it was requisitioned

Westcliffe House lies behind the Lee-on-the-Solent war memorial, just inside the perimeter wall of the former Daedalus *military base. (LM)*

for the military in 1917 for the new seaplane training base and used as officers' quarters.

The acres of land behind the seafront in West Lee were still sparsely developed and subsequently became the additional Royal Naval Air Service seaplane training school. The seaplane base was only expected to be a First World War expedient, but after the war and with the completion of a new slipway, the Royal Flying Corps and Royal Naval Air Service jointly operated from Lee, turning it into a permanent station. The two services subsequently combined to form the Royal Air Force, located at RAF Lee-on-Solent (this was the first official use of the short name form for Lee).

In May 1939, the base returned to Admiralty control and was commissioned as one of His Majesty's shore bases, HMS *Daedalus*. Fortunately, this protected Westcliffe House from significant change behind the military fence as well as keeping it in use and maintained. Thus, it remains one of the less-adapted original seafront properties, justifiably one of Lee's listed buildings.

MILITARY EXPANSION

The seaplane hangars were among the earliest First World War structures erected on the site, located on two sides of a generous concrete apron – Seaplane Square – and eventually connected by a concrete slipway to the sea. The military soon began to shape the site with its own powerhouse in 1918, adding additional requisitioned buildings and farmland of West Lee. Roads and houses predating 1917 were either demolished or reused, the most notable among these is Westcliffe House.

A major expansion was undertaken after 1931, when the base became the Coastal Command HQ. The most architecturally distinguished building relating to this phase is the Officers' Mess or Wardroom, now Grade-II listed. It was completed in 1935, at a time when the liaison between the government and the Royal Fine Arts Commission resulted in a high-quality design for important military buildings. It fronts onto a large, grassed area to its south, with views over The Solent. On the town side, it is bounded by a group of former married quarters in the garden-city style, which is characteristic of RAF expansion up to 1934. To the north is the station guardhouse (a 1926 design), accommodation and the barracks square of 1932–35.

Rapid expansion for the Second World War required runways on which to train aircrew for carrier operations and subsequently for the many land-based aircraft that defended us in our 'darkest hour' during the Battle of

New-build houses adjacent to the runway at Solent Airport are indicative of modern redevelopment patterns on former Ministry of Defence sites. (LM)

Britain. As well as extra land, further additions included the H-plan barracks blocks and Eagle Block, which served as the HQ of Coastal Command.

On D-Day, 435 sorties were flown from the base, the highest total of any of the UK airfields. This military expansion took a big bite out of the western development lands of Lee. This militarisation development was very different from that envisaged by the town's founding fathers. All this expansion was without any regard for the original resort town-planning concept. The extra settlement 'behind the wire' insulated it from civilian planning requirements. Nonetheless, the significant expansion of servicemen and women also brought the need for a greater range of Lee shops and services, prompting a shift from the focus of supporting the wealthy property owner to supporting the more balanced requirements of a 'new town' community.

DEVELOPMENT BETWEEN THE WARS

The interwar years saw the greatest period of the town's development. The pressing requirement to build homes brought in resident builders, a solicitor and architect and, with the increasing population, a doctor and dentist. Newcomers also needed services, not just food but clothing and hardware. There was even a garage to service the new motor car.

Beyond the residential increase, air races, and particularly the Schneider Trophy events of 1927 and 1929, really put Lee on the tourist map. Not just for those who could afford to come by car and picnic on the clifftop, the new railway also drew in people and, to their delight, they found the beach, pier and modern attractions. Lee could claim it was really growing, adding to its ever-increasing military population and becoming popular for day trippers. This all required better services to add to the early and more limited infrastructure.

The Estate Company still ran many services but on a meagre budget. Their patched roads were one of the many ratepayers' complaints. Eventually the district council adopted and made up some of the roads but by the 1920s, Lee ratepayers wanted responsible services and not a feigned interest from Crofton Parish. There was an additional confusion – who was actually responsible for the provision of local services? Stubbington, Fareham and Gosport all 'looked after' parts of Lee. Should it be adopted as an urban or rural council? Lee residents favoured Gosport, while Fareham and the district council all thought it would be prestigious to have a seaside resort and a military base on the books. By 1 April 1930, Lee-on-the-Solent became part of Gosport Borough, although wrangling about roads, drainage and other services went on for much longer.

DEVELOPMENTS 1930 PLUS – ART DECO AND BEYOND

The 1930s heralded other entrepreneurs, who rebuilt the pier and the Lee Tower in a visually bold art deco style, prompting other art deco development in the locality. Eric Andrews' and Cyril Bagley's designs of art deco houses on Milvil Road, with flat roofs and metal-framed windows, were cutting-edge style for the time. They have become classic examples of the building form to this day.

Local architect Trevor Tatham, later a Lee alderman, designed several buildings in Lee High Street, Pier Street and opposite the Tower complex. His Portsmouth Road houses were variations of art deco with castellated roof parapets.

However, not all development was art deco, as the majority of builders continued in the traditional pitch roof and red-brick style. To this traditional building some variety was added by exposed wood framing and interwar features, such as bay windows and pebble dash or painted renders.

All a facade? Lee seafront is characterised by residential frontages of many different architectural styles and hues. (LM)

June 1933 also saw the opening of St Faith's Parish Church as a replacement for the former tin church on Victoria Square bequeathed by the Robinson family. While not art deco, it was modernist with its series of bold internal catenary concrete arches to support the building. Similar side aisles are of a sharper, more defined arch shape. Together, they give a sense of a strong, uplifted space ideal for worship. These rectangular arches were cast in situ and were innovative in design and workmanship for the 1930s, if not the best for the internal acoustics.

Currently the church, a listed building, is undergoing its first major exterior repairs since it was first built, with features like the mansard roof dormer windows needing their wooden frames replaced to make them weathertight again. Equally, the tired interior needs a makeover, and a sound survey has indicated that modern sound-absorbent finishes can improve the acoustic reflections without any changes in the essential design character. Unsurprisingly, these works to a listed building are way beyond the means of the congregation, or the town for that matter! So, progress is slow, yet important, as the church is one of the few listed buildings in Lee that are still in daily use.

POST-SECOND WORLD WAR EXPANSION

The Second World War halted development and a few houses were destroyed in air attacks, not unsurprisingly scattered around the town as HMS *Daedalus* could put up an effective air defence. Returning heavy anti-aircraft shells caused local casualties – ten members of the Women's Royal Naval Service (WRENS), in their billet in Newton Place, and the Reverend Douglas Hunter, in St Faith's Vicarage, all died as a result of returning anti-aircraft shells.

The post-war replacement housing added variety in style to the street scene. The houses were no longer of grand proportions and were needed urgently, resulting in the division of some of the original plots and incremental infilling with smaller houses and bungalows. Nonetheless, these smaller properties remained true to the original street layout.

The war also heralded the immediacy of post-war prefabricated homes. Once the base was completed, the structure could be erected in about two hours. These were built around Elmore Avenue. Prefabricated homes were not as unpopular as might be expected, because insulation and energy efficiency were not concerns of the day. On the contrary, an interior bathroom and lavatory, an all-electric fit-out, including a refrigerator, were cutting edge for the time and were popular. None of these homes remain, but have been replaced by single-storey dwellings evident in a few rows of similar houses around the Elmore area.

Contrastingly, the airbase remained predominant in the west of the town but added to the residential street pattern with distinctive RAF-style married quarters, just outside the base and further afield in Hill Head.

Modern development needs little explanation. On the seafront, most of the grand Victorian and Edwardian mansions have been lost to high-rise flat development, driven by the need for more housing and the developers' wish to maximise the profit with multi-occupancy living. Even the few seafront Edwardian buildings that remain are all multi-occupancy, sometimes divided to as many as six or eight apartments.

A seafront planning guidance document, drafted by the successor to the ratepayers' body, the Lee Residents Association, was adopted by the council in 2007. This has helped to save some of the character by restricting the height of seafront buildings and specifying pitched roofs and breaks in long slab frontages in its design guidelines. Sadly, many residents would argue that its effectiveness is being constantly challenged and its efficacy diminished by the constant clamour for profitability.

Developers usually prefer to demolish in favour of multi-occupancy flats. Where houses are updated, even under the design guidance, utilising clapboard finishes and all-glass frontages right up to the roof apex provides a stylistic inclusion, if not always the most weatherproof facades. Long gone are the days when the original developers, the Robinson family, could dictate what was built as a mark of good taste for their resort.

The conversion or replacement of the larger houses has started to creep back from the seafront, prompting the Lee Residents Association to draft another design guidance document for West Lee, adopted by GBC in 2019. Hopefully, this twenty-first-century design guidance will help maintain more of the original character of Lee behind its seafront and resist some of the interplot or garden-grabbing developments as well as profit-seeking, high-rise growth.

Google Earth satellite view still evidences the characteristics of Victorian 'new town' planning, with a grid-type layout around the original centre of the church, and on the street there is still a marked absence of workers' houses near the town centre, except as flats over the shops. Nowhere are there any Victorian back-to-back terrace rows that are so common to the Victorian industrial town.

An art deco enclave in Milvil Road. The fairly short-lived architectural movement of the 1930s left its mark here in Lee and in other parts of the town, including the shopping terrace at West Point and the Lee Tower and Ballroom complex of 1935 (long since demolished). (LM)

SO, WHAT FOR THE FUTURE?

This brings us to the modern era. We don't always think of cars as supporting a change in Lee, just a parking problem. But as cars became more widely available, the modern residential housing estate made its appearance in East Lee with the development of the Cherque Farm Estate. This edge-of-town development would not be viable without many of its residents using multi-car ownership to commute out to work and shop.

Ironically, this returns us to one of the Robinsons' earliest problems, the lack of easy access to Fareham and beyond. Although the connecting roads now exist, they have become overburdened and need improvement again. The Newgate Lane relief road (recently opened) and the Stubbington bypass (at the time of writing under construction), are essential to restore reasonable journey times.

The down side? The strip of strategic gap on either side of the new roads is a magnet to the greenfield developer, irrespective of the implication of undoing the traffic improvements the new roads were designed to provide. Perhaps this road congestion also encourages the trend to online shopping and delivery – better to let someone else brave the queues!

Contrastingly, part of West Lee was held in a time warp from 1986 when the military moved out and preserved all that was left behind the wire of the abandoned HMS *Daedalus*. Fortunately, some of the original buildings the military left behind are listed and within a Daedalus Conservation area, although the lack of any maintenance makes them very expensive to reuse. For the part that has a sea frontage, it would be ideal if there was another Robinson-style entrepreneur looking for quality rather than the 'turn a quick profit' developer.

As mentioned, investment developers favour high-rise, multi-occupancy mini-flats, selling at a premium for their Solent sea view. This type of development is already present and some of it is a sad legacy of the lack of planning insight of the 1960s–1990s. Pier Street and the town centre, a conservation area since March 2009, has helped retain some of the historical content and architectural style of the very centre of Lee significantly, including the Grade-II-listed Le Breton Farmhouse, which dates from the fourteenth century.

Today, as West Lee re-emerges from 'military service', the operational airfield and its hangars provide the ideal location for surrounding the airfield with hi-tech and aeronautical industry, aided by a government-supported economic zone. This has the duel aim of providing economic growth and local employment to help reduce the daily out-commuting congestion.

Smaller estate development homes within the former administrative area of *Daedalus* should help with this aim. To integrate this modern development, some of the historical buildings are being retained and new flats and housing are designed to be in 'sympathetic similarity' to nearby buildings in the conservation area. The listed buildings should remain, but the years of neglect place a heavy burden on cost-effective conversion.

VISION AND COMMUNITY COMMITMENT REQUIRED

Is there a modern-day John Robinson out there to come in with vision and money to shape the missing section of Lee town to the west of the church? There may be! A new player in the game, the Daedalus Development Corporation, has, in 2022, taken commercial responsibility (in collaboration with Homes England and local municipal authorities) for those as yet undeveloped areas around Seaplane Square on the Solent Airport estate. Their expressed vision includes not just additional new commercial and residential property, following the now complete Wates Company houses, east and west of the Hovercraft Museum and the Daedalus Park industrial estate, which faces the active airfield, but also a commitment to the retention, revitalisation and enhancement of the Hovercraft Museum to national exhibition standards under conditions of improved tenure and sustainable funding arrangements.

9

THE RESTORATION OF NO. 5 GRANGE FARM

Robert Whiteley

The residential property known as Grange Farm is located just to the west of the built-up area of Gosport. The indicative drawing of Grange Farm by Ronald Paffard appeared on the cover of *Gosport Records*, a publication of The Gosport Society, in November 1972. That edition included an article by Elizabeth Haughton. She described the property as a 'sorry spectacle of neglect'. Grange Farm had to wait another six years before owners GBC decided to restore the old house and its adjacent farm buildings.

No. 5 Grange Farm – a historic property in the Alver Valley. (LM)

The farmhouse was divided into three separate dwellings. The south wing, on the left in the drawing (which is the oldest part of the house), formed one dwelling. Just over half of the central section, including a staircase tower, formed a second dwelling. The rest of the original timber-framed central section and the north wing formed the third dwelling. This is known as No. 5 Grange Farm.

The three newly formed dwellings were let to people who worked for GBC. They all, under the housing legislation of the day, exercised their right as 'sitting tenants' to buy their houses. When we were buying 5 Grange Farm, the surveyor stated that technically he had to describe the property as 'a three-bedroomed, end-of-terrace ex council house' – true! But not the whole truth. It would have been more accurate if he had added 'almost certainly extended and modernised nearly 450 years ago'.

HISTORICAL NOTES

It is believed that Grange Farm was built by monks from Quarr Abbey (on the Isle of Wight, between Ryde and Cowes) in or around 1295. Following the Dissolution of the Monasteries in 1538, the property was acquired by Sir John Brune, whose fine monument stands in the family chapel of the Church of St Mary the Virgin, Rowner, just a mile or so north of Grange Farm.

Sir John's son, Henry, moved to Athelhampton House in Dorset and the farm was let to tenants. However, the property remained in the ownership of the Brune/Prideaux-Brune combined families for almost 400 years. Formal records show that in the time of King Edward I, a manor of Rowner was created and granted to Sir William Le Brun in 1277, in 'grateful thanks' for loyal martial service in the Anglo–Scottish Wars.

St Mary the Virgin in Rowner became the manor church. Two of Sir William's sons, Philip and Nicholas Le Brun, were instituted as the first rectors from 1292. Their names head a continuous list of fifty-five rectors down the centuries listed on the slate in the church vestibule. Over time, the Brune family and their offshoots, the Prideaux-Brunes, offered patronages, retained farmlands and exercised manorial direction, increasingly from their additional estates in the West Country.

A survey in 1800 and a map of 1802 of the whole manor of Rowner show that Grange Farm consisted of 696 acres. In 1857, the War Department compulsory purchased 430 acres of the Prideaux-Brune manor, which included 318 acres of Grange Farm. This land was needed for the construction of Fort

Grange and Fort Rowner, which formed part of a chain of forts built to protect Portsmouth Harbour.

In 1914, the Royal Flying Corps took over vacant land around Forts Grange and Rowner for one of its first seven RFC airfields, which were to play a vital role in the First World War. In 1925, the War Department bought all that remained of Grange Farm to extend the Grange Airfield site. This made an important contribution to UK air defence in the Second World War and beyond. In 1956, parts of the airfield were converted into the present HMS *Sultan*, a shore establishment of the Royal Navy.

Manorial landholdings surrounding Grange Farm finally passed from the Brune dynasty in 1948, to accommodate (under post-Second World War government rehousing policies) the large housing estates that are such a striking feature of the Rowner and Bridgemary areas today. However, surviving members of the Brune/Prideau-Brune family retain a prerogative in the beneficc institution of rectors at St Mary the Virgin. Grange Farm, once the agricultural epicentre of the former manorial lands associated with the church, has indeed a long and influential pedigree.

THE RESTORATION AFTER 1997

Floor plans (below) show the ground-floor layout of 5 Grange Farm when we first moved into the house in 1997 and subsequently after restoring it to as near as possible its original layout. Dotted lines on the pre-1997 plan show all the old oak ceiling beams. These had been left exposed in the earlier (1978) restoration. The later plan shows the additional ceiling beams we uncovered. Also, marked in black are some of the timber framings in the walls that had been plastered over.

The restoration in 1978 had used plasterboard partitions to divide the two large rooms at the front of the house into seven different areas. We removed more than 40ft of plasterboard partitioning while restoring these two rooms to their original dimensions. We found that all the timber framing in the former central portion of the house had been covered in plaster, as had an oak door frame and window lintels. Plasterboard had also been used to cover oak beams in parts of the ceiling.

The fireplace had been reduced in size over many generations, from the original 8ft by 4ft to 3ft by 2ft. GBC had, at some time, added a course of modern bricks painted a bright red. We had to remove five separate walls from the back of the fireplace to reach the original back wall. We also had to remove a side pillar that probably dated from Victorian times.

The old fireplace with some modern bricks removed from the left pillar. The Victorian pillar on the right was flanked by a plasterboard partition between the lounge and the long staircase cupboard, part of which has been removed. (RW)

Most of the restored wall between the lounge in the former timber-framed central section of the house, and beyond it, looking to the dining hall in the north wing. All these wall timbers had been covered with modern plaster, which we removed. The brick infill between the timber frames had obviously never meant to be shown, so the wall was replastered, leaving all the timber frames exposed. (RW)

Removing a worn-out log-burning stove and a concrete shelf above it revealed the enormous chimney, stretching the full width of the fireplace. It had iron brackets placed at intervals to facilitate climbing and cleaning the chimney.

The 1997 floor plan shows that between the lounge and the stairs there was a long, narrow cupboard. The stairs were made of poor timber and we decided to have a completely new oak staircase fitted. As built, this was modelled on a sixteenth-century staircase in one of the heritage buildings at the Open-Air Downland Musem in Singleton, West Sussex. Doing away with the cupboard and replacing a half-landing with three-quarter-turn stairs allowed us to open up a corner of the room.

The fireplace, restored as near as possible to its original size. The pillar on the left had to remain because it supports the next-door bathroom. A corner of the new staircase is visible at the top right of this picture. (RW)

The 1997 floor plan also shows an area between the utility room and the inner hall. This appeared to be a solid square with a space either side behind a thin wall. We found that the wall was, in fact, sheets of plasterboard that had been used to hide a solid brick pillar, 2ft square and reaching from floor to ceiling but supporting nothing. Either side of it were empty spaces also about 2ft square. During the restoration, this previously hidden area has been increased by taking 1ft from the utility room and the brick pillar has been completely removed. Bricks from this area were reused to form the floor of the restored fireplace in the lounge. The brick-filled timber-frame wall so revealed was also restored. A new toilet and washbasin were installed to replace the old ones removed from the area next to the front door.

All this is very obvious when you enter the house. It is not so obvious that we also had to replace two-thirds of the windows. The frames and sills were rotted. Since this is a Grade-II-listed building, all of these had to be handmade to match the original windows. The back door was also rotten and a handmade replacement fitted.

Some of the very large sixteenth- or seventeenth-century oak roofing timbers had been badly infested by beetles and damaged by wet or dry rot because there was no ventilation in the area. As well as treating all the timbers, several new struts and supported purlins were installed. It was also necessary to strengthen one area with steel brackets and plates. Finally, special ventilation tiles were installed. (RW)

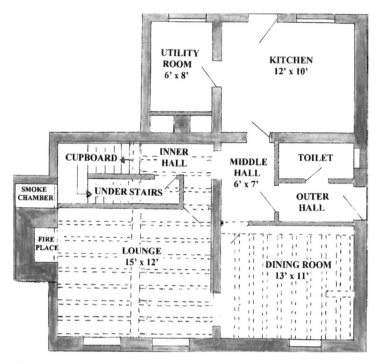

The floor plan prior to restoration. (RW)

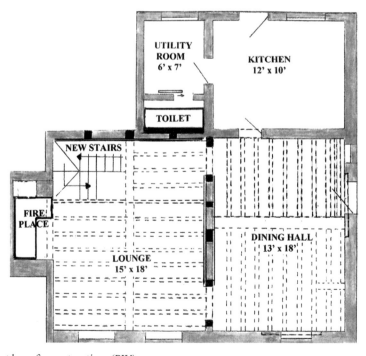

The floor plan after restoration. (RW)

The north wall of the dining room was found to be very damp. On the exterior wall, the bricks and mortar of a disused chimney stack were saturated. The chimney pot at the top of the stack had been left open, allowing rainwater to enter. Thus, the chimney placed there as part of the 1978 restoration had become a 25ft-tall 'reservoir' feeding the rising damp affecting the wall. The inside wall along the whole length of the dining room had to be stripped of plaster from floor to ceiling, treated with damp-proofing material and replastered. The solid brick wall was drilled externally and a damp-proof course installed by pressure injection. The top 5ft of the chimney stack and the chimney pot were removed, the chimney suitably capped and two air bricks installed.

A labour of love? Certainly! But worth it, as the house has been referred to as 'Gosport's medieval treasure'. To us, it is just home and we love it!

10

KEEPING TRACK: GOSPORT RAILWAYS AND THEIR URBAN LEGACY

Peter Keat

GOSPORT RAILWAY STATION IN 1841

The decision to locate a railway and related station on the Gosport peninsula originated in intense rivalry between the towns of Portsmouth and Southampton. With the passing of the London & Southampton Railway Company (LSRC) Act of 1834, establishing the Portsmouth Satellite Railway Company, a proposal emerged to construct a main line to Portsmouth from Bishopstoke (Eastleigh). Portsmouth residents at that time objected strongly to any company that had the name Southampton in the title. Similarly, Portsmouth Town Council would not allow the construction of the line into Portsmouth. All this before the days of football rivalry! Another complication was that outer fortifications meant the line would have to stop at Hilsea, preventing the railway from reaching Portsea Island itself.

The site on which the station was built was formerly an orchard and fields owned by a local landowner, Mr Isaac Legg. Work had already started on the line from the Southampton end, the contractors being Thomas Brassey and the engineer Joseph Locke. On reaching Fareham, the line faced an impasse. The Portsmouth objections were lodged, so a plan was confirmed to build the line to Gosport instead, this route giving access to Portsmouth via a cross-harbour ferry link. By this time, the London & Southampton Railway had already been taken over by the London & South Western Railway (LSWR), so part of the Portsmouth argument about the Southampton connection no longer pertained.

There were also defence-related difficulties at Gosport, but here the fortified ramparts were closer to the town centre. The commanding officer's refusal to let his walls be breached was strategically of little importance, but the station was near enough to service Royal Clarence Yard, the nearby Royal Navy victualling yard, and the station did not interfere with lines of fire from the town ramparts.

The line from Fareham into Gosport faced very little in the way of engineering complexity. But the section through the South Downs, just north of Fareham was a different matter. The line was due to open on 26 July 1841 but a landslip caused by unstable soil and rock conditions in a tunnel near Fareham caused a delay.

The line was eventually opened on 29 November 1841. The first train was hauled from Nine Elms (London) to Gosport by locomotive No. 17, *Queen*. The locomotive was new that year and the train consisted of four first-class carriages. It took three and a half hours to complete the journey.

However, the line was closed only four days later because of a further landslip in a tunnel north of Fareham, and reopened again on 7 February 1842. The only way that the contractors could solve this problem of tunnel collapse was to excavate the landslip out and create two separate tunnels, one much shorter than the other. These two tunnels are still in daily use some 180 years later.

Gosport's former Victorian railway station was restored with the classical facade retained. (LM)

This was the start of the railways on the peninsula of Gosport. In its heyday, the peninsula had nine working stations; four branch lines (Lee-on-the-Solent, Stokes Bay, Royal Clarence Yard and the Royal Naval Armaments Depot Frater); one commercial miniature railway with its own station; a narrow-gauge beach, wind and man-powered railway; plus a manually operated narrow-gauge target railway on the army ranges. This is not counting a temporary track on the Stokes Bay line, which was put in to supply extracted ballast. Much of the ballast for the newly constructed Meon Valley line was drawn from here. Much later, after the Second World War, light narrow-gauge railways were frequently moved on and around building sites in the Gosport area. They were often manned by prisoners of war until they were repatriated.

The construction costs of the line were £404,271 – over £12,000 more than the original estimate. The Gosport Station building itself was designed by William Tite (later Sir William), the celebrated designer of the Royal Exchange in London. The station design is of an Italianate, classic tradition, which was very popular at that time, and was finished with Tuscan columns with Corinthian capitals. It was built by Mr Nicholson at a total cost of £10,980. By way of comparison, Fareham Station only cost £1,3921. A modern block of apartments in Gosport has been named Tite Court, so keeping the name in the public mind.

A tank engine typical of those of the London and South Western Railway that daily worked the Gosport railways in the days of steam. (GSA)

During the early years, fast trains to London were limited by law to 20mph. The single fare was 22s on the fast service, but there was also a slow third-class stopping service with open carriages that cost only 8s 6d. Mixed trains of first- and second-class carriages were also run and charged at the rate of 21s for first class and 15s for second class. The line was unfortunate enough to suffer from early vandalism when, in 1842, two juveniles received sentences of imprisonment from the Gosport Magistrates, one of one month and the other of three months, for throwing stones at trains.

The royal connection with Gosport Station began on 8 October 1843 when Prince Albert came by train to greet HM Louis-Phillipe, King of France. The first recorded visit to Gosport Station by Queen Victoria came six days later, when she accompanied the king on his return to France.

Travelling down the line from Fareham, the first branch encountered led off to the Royal Naval Armaments Depot at Frater*, and the older gunpowder factory at Priddy's Hard. It was here that munitions, ordnance and explosives were manufactured and stored prior to redistribution to ships of the Royal Navy and to armed services bases elsewhere in the United Kingdom.

The actual date of the laying of the first section of track within the munitions depots of Gosport would appear to be sometime before 1883. This can be deduced from an article in a May 1883 edition of the *Hampshire Telegraph*. This describes the use of a narrow-gauge railway for the movement of armaments into the earth- and turf-protected magazines at the depots. At this time, it would appear that all the magazines were connected and serviced by this railway, One must now assume that the lines were built sometime before this article was published, probably about forty years earlier, when the Royal Naval Laboratories were established in Priddy's Hard. As a consequence of the production of munitions, a safe and efficient method of transporting shells and explosives between the filling rooms and the magazines had to be found. It is logical then to assume that the system was first installed between 1848 and 1851.

It appears that there was not one but two narrow-gauge systems in the munitions yards come the turn of the twentieth century. We learn from a departmental report of 1904 that two manually operated narrow-gauge railways were in use, one of 1ft 6in gauge and the other 2ft 6in. To reduce the risk of sparks, the rails of the smaller-gauge line were made of a copper alloy. The wheels of the wagons, some seventy to eighty in number, were treated

* The location for a huge explosion of an ammunition barge in 1951. The Frater site is still operational and is now known as Defence Munitions Gosport (DMG).

in the same way. The whole system was single track except for shunting sidings for collection and deliveries.

To date, there is no information on any form of motive power on the smaller-gauge line apart from human muscle power. This was not so on the 2ft 6in-gauge system. This eventually superseded the narrower one. The broader gauge used twenty to thirty wagons. Their larger size meant that not as many were required as on the narrower system.

In 1929, two battery rail tractors were purchased from Greenwood and Batley. They proved to be so successful that over the next year six more were bought. All the tractors worked until the system closed in 1960. These locomotives were equipped with flameproof motors, controllers and switchgear. However, they were not allowed to work into the explosive stores and workshops, where manual power still remained supreme. These locomotives weighed only 56cwt and cost £690 when new – and this included delivery.

The battery tractors were replaced in 1960 by road tractor units. When this transfer was complete, the rail system was closed.

The standard-gauge line worked right up to 1990, from its first beginnings in 1912. During the early years after the railway first came to Gosport, the depot(s) would collect armaments stores from Gosport Station using a horse and cart. However, when it was realised what an advantage a direct rail connection could be, the Admiralty approached the LSWR with a view to laying in an approach siding from the Gosport main line to the depot at Frater. This was in 1910.

The projected cost of this extension was £638 and the Admiralty would also be liable for 10 per cent of the expenditure on the line for the next twenty-five years. The terms were agreeable to the Admiralty and work on the extension began in early 1911. The required official Board of Trade inspection was conducted on 20 January 1912.

Access to the Frater connection was from the main line at a point near Oakdene. Here, the extension curved off to the east, then crossed the Gosport–Fareham road (A32) and went on into the depot.* The original layout of the system at Frater is unknown. There have been so many land use changes and alterations over the years that it is almost impossible to be certain about the configuration of the original line. However, it is known that the network extended outside the confines of the Frater depot when

---

* The former standard-gauge extension line into the Frater RNAD now forms part of the dedicated E1 and E2 bus route, running between Fareham and Gosport. See the contemporary photograph on page 126.

a single line was laid to the magazine depot at Priddy's Hard. The modern road of Heritage Way is in part constructed over this line.

The standard-gauge line was always locomotive worked. The first of these were built by Andrew Barclay & Co. Over the years, Barclay & Co. supplied no fewer than nine locomotives, the first being *Bedenham* No. 1, which was an 0-4-0 fireless locomotive. The series of fireless engines supplied to the yard worked on a charged reservoir pressure of 160 Ihs/sq. Steam was provided by one of the boiler houses on site. During an average working day, the reservoirs would be charged first thing, there would then be enough steam to last until lunchtime. They would then be charged again, this being enough to complete the working day. The livery of these locomotives was light green with lined panels and vermilion buffers.

LESSER-KNOWN RAILWAY TALES

On 24 April 1987, a rather embarrassing shunting accident occurred to the morning Frater goods train. Stones in the points caused a derailment. Normally the area would be well covered by MoD Police but once this happened they all disappeared, which resulted in a rather unique photograph of a toddler trying to climb into an explosives wagon through the broken door on the other side.

***

The first station on the line was Fort Brockhurst. This is as old as the line itself and was furnished with not only a signal box and level crossing, but accommodation for the resident station master. Here was the junction to the independent Lee-on-the-Solent Railway. The access to this line was via a shunt from the up main line. Brockhurst Station was kept busy in respect of the military personal stationed at Fort Grange, HMS *Siskin* and Fort Brockhurst. It was also featured in the 1955 film *Cockleshell Heroes*, when the line was taken over by the film company for a complete Sunday (the line was closed on Sundays at this time) to film a 30-second section of film.

***

On 21 November 1952, Queen Elizabeth alighted from the royal train at the station on her way to visit HMS *Ariel* at Lee-on-the-Solent. In the local schools it was announced that the pupils would line the road by the station

A ticket to ride – to see HM the Queen.

that morning and they could have the rest of the day off. One enterprising young lad, the previous evening, hid his fishing rod in the bushes by the moat so he could go fishing the next afternoon. As the motorcade passed the pupils, this particular lad shouted out 'good old Queen!', little knowing that his headmaster was standing behind him. The rest of the day went well for him but the next morning he was called to the headmaster's office, where he received six of the best for disrespecting the queen.

LEE-ON-THE-SOLENT

In 1894 a branch line was extended to Lee-on-the-Solent. It was never a commercial success and failed to pay a dividend to its shareholders. It lasted only forty-one years. Passenger traffic was withdrawn in 1931 and the last freight train ran in 1935.

Both the Stokes Bay line (which branched off further into town), and the Lee-on-the-Solent Railway were originally built by independent companies. They were eventually taken over by the larger LSWR, who ran the London–Gosport main line.

Where once the railways ran. The former terminus station platform edge was revealed when a new children's playground was installed on the beachfront at Lee-on-the-Solent. Note the preserved facade of the once-grand Pier Hotel in the background. The hotel was part of the drive to create a new seaside resort in Lee. It is now a luxury apartment building. (LM)

Over 125 years ago, Sir John Robinson had a vision of the fishing and farming village of Lee-on-the-Solent becoming a major south coast seaside resort. To this end, he planned land-use changes that included improving the transport system in the area. A pier was planned to improve the access by water, new roads were laid out in a grid pattern and a new railway was planned to connect Lee-on-the-Solent with the Gosport to Fareham line at Fort Brockhurst. There was also a proposed Fareham Railway Act, which sought to build a line from Fareham through Stubbington to Lee. That never happened.

It was the original intention of the Lee-on-the-Solent Railway Company to own and run its own locomotives. There was, however, never a plan for an engine shed or workshops. The plan seems to have been dropped very early, on cost grounds. We soon read of various negotiations between the LSRC and the LSWR for the hire of locomotives to work the line. An agreement between the companies was eventually reached and a 2-4-0 side tank loco-motive – *Scott* – was transferred to the line in time to work the inaugural train. Work on the line then alternated between *Scott* and an even smaller locomotive, the 0-6-0 *Lady Portsmouth*.

The services got under way with eight trains in each direction daily and three in each direction on a Sunday. But take a look at the 1908 timetable and note that the first train from Lee-on-the-Solent in the morning ran at 9.20 a.m. and the first train from Fort Brockhurst left at 10.15 a.m. Hardly a convenient timetable for the average working man! And there was a service on a Sunday only until the afternoon.

In 1914 this all changed to ten trains in each direction daily, the first leaving Fort Brockhurst at 8.55 a.m. and the last arriving there at 8.47 p.m. There was only a Sunday service in July.

Passenger accommodation was fairly primitive. Early years carriage stock consisted only of old four-wheeled coaches, which ran very badly and had a tendency to become derailed. Later on, the company tried unsuccessfully to use a rail-motor, which was a locomotive and carriage combined. This did not work, so a conversion of the rail-motor coach section to serve passenger purposes was undertaken. The coach had an American tramway profile with a wrought-iron balcony at the front and back of the coach and an entrance in the middle of the carriage, which was protected by a metal grille with a folding iron gate. To complete the tramway illusion, the slatted wooden seats were lined against the sides of the coach under the windows from front to back and not sideways.

After the line was closed, the actual rails and sleepers remained in place along part of the route until well into the Second World War. There is a reported incident that a pilot from HMS *Siskin* (now HMS *Sultan*) overshot the runway and 'pranged his crate' on the old railway line, causing much damage to his plane. In his defence, when he was called before the commanding officer, he claimed that it was all the old railway's fault because if they had removed the rails the damage would have not been so severe!

STOKES BAY

In 1863, a branch line was opened via a connecting triangle on the main line about half a mile from the main Gosport Station (see the contemporary photograph on page 124). This ran to Stokes Bay, where it joined up with a ferry link to Ryde, on the Isle of Wight. The ferries on this service ceased in spring 1914 and the rail link was withdrawn on 30 October 1915. However, the pier remained for many years after closure and for some time was used by the Admiralty as a torpedo testing station.

It was never the intention of the Stokes Bay Railway and Pier Company (SBRPC) to provide locomotives and rolling stock. It was hoped that the LSWR would work the line for them at an agreed rate. At a November 1865 meeting, it was decided that the funds of the SBRPC were so limited that the LSWR would have to work the line at cost price to try to stem the ever-increasing drain on SBPRC company finances. Reluctantly, the LSWR agreed to work the line but insisted on certain improvements being made. By March (1866) figures of over £40,000 were being quoted for the work and the negotiations with the contractors were at a standstill. No agreement could be reached with engineers Smith & Knight, so they retired from the scene and devoted their energies to building the Metropolitan Railway instead.

Contrary to popular belief, there is no recorded incident of Queen Victoria sailing to the Isle of Wight from the pier at Stokes Bay. However, there is an account of her landing there on a very foggy night when the royal yacht could not safely sail into Portsmouth Harbour and on to the landing place in Royal Clarence Yard. The fact that she did not use Stokes Bay is not surprising as one cannot help thinking that Her Majesty would have been far from 'amused' by the exposed position, the strength of the wind and the occasional roughness of the sea if she had travelled this way. G.P. Neale, who attended the queen on most of her railway journeys between Osborne and Balmoral, reports in his own private papers that she travelled only to her own private pier in Gosport at Royal Clarence Yard. He does refer in several places, though, to the royal household luggage travelling to and from the island via another route – Stokes Bay.

Even without royal patronage, the Stokes Bay line for many years conveyed thousands of happy trippers over to the Isle of Wight. This continued until the opening of the station at Portsmouth Harbour in 1876. The introduction of a ferry service from that station to Ryde was the death knell for the line, which had been known as the 'Family Route' to the Isle of Wight.

Very few stories are told about the line and the pier, but I understand that part of the pier was made over as a boathouse, and a boat, on fine summer evenings, was used for short fishing trips, all strictly against regulations, of course. Fishing from this boat was all very well, but during the winter months it was most uncomfortable. I well remember an ex-Gosport Station employee telling me that the permanent staff on the pier had cut, and made a cover for, a hole in the ticket office floor so that they could drop a line down in inclement weather. I understand that the sea underneath the pier was a favourite resting place for various forms of flat fish. So, one can imagine on a cold winter's night, while walking along the shoreline, the local residents could catch the waft of the smell of shallow fried fish as the station staff cooked their ill-gained supper on the small stove in the ticket office. A nice story but how true is it?

Another story about the branch line that I can vouch for comes from a long-time resident, Elizabeth Belben. The Belben family had moved into Gosport in 1893. They first moved into a house in Leonard Road, where they paid the equivalent of 25p a week rent for a three-bedroom house with a front room, kitchen and scullery. They moved from there in 1901 into a house in Camden Street and eventually settled into rented accommodation in Kings Road. This district was originally called Bingham Town after a past incumbent of the Parish of Holy Trinity. This area was originally brickfields and orchards, and was formerly served by a horse tram and later an electric tram service along Stoke Road.

Harry Belben and his wife (Elizabeth's parents) took in a lodger. This was railway guard Tom Belben, Harry's cousin. Tom was a railway servant in the grade of Passenger Guard and was of many years' seniority. Being based at Gosport Station, Guard Belben was very often rostered to work as guard on the local Eastleigh–Fareham–Gosport–Stokes Bay train, down to the pier and back. This was a regular service taking passengers from London via a slip coach, which was detached at Eastleigh.

Each week day there was always a train that returned from Stokes Bay Pier to Gosport, arriving just after midday. When this train had discharged its passengers and been put into the yard to be serviced and unloaded of its goods traffic (not a long task as the line at this period of time was never very busy), the train crew would take their lunch breaks.

Elizabeth Belben told very graphically of the way that the guard's dinner was set on the table whenever he was on duty aboard this train. Being well known in the area and knowing most of the engine crews, Guard Belben was normally able to persuade the driver to give a whistle as he approached the back of Kings Road. This is what Mrs Belben was waiting for. On hearing this whistle, she would know that very soon her lodger would be home, hungry for his dinner, and she would begin to dish it up. So, by the time the train had been dealt with and the guard had walked to his home, Mrs Belben had served up the meal and his dinner was sitting on the table ready. Nice!

Lodgers were common during this period of history. It was a good way to make ends meet and it was common to let out a spare room to someone who needed a home. The Belbens were no exception. For example, Ernie North lodged with the Belbens around 1893. He was another railway guard and, like Guard Belben, often worked the Stokes Bay trains. At this period of time, a guards' pay was only about 15s a week. Out of his pay, Mr North would pay Mrs Belben 10s a week. This was to pay for his room, meals, washing and clothes mending.

With pay in mind, it is worth mentioning that when Elizabeth Belben's brother began work at Gosport Station in the early 1900s as an office boy, his pay was 10s a week. Of this amount, he paid his mother 5s a week for his keep and he was allowed to keep 5s for himself. The amounts of money seem, to the modern reader, ridiculously small but the cost of living then was lower.

THE ROYAL CLARENCE YARD CONNECTION

In 1846, the renovation of Osborne House at Cowes, on the Isle of Wight, was completed. Upon remembering her previous trip to Gosport, Queen Victoria requested that the ramparts be opened. This royal request was one that the commanding officer of the Gosport Garrison readily agreed to! Thus, a 600-yard rail extension was laid into the Royal Clarence Yard where the Royal Victoria Station was built. Its partial remains are currently in the ownership of UK Docks Ltd. Its future is currently to be determined but the tunnel through the ramparts is still in place.

A FUNERAL OF NATIONAL SIGNIFICANCE

With the death of Queen Victoria on 22 January 1901 at Osborne House, funeral plans had to be made quickly. Even the royal undertakers, Buntings of London, were unprepared for a royal funeral. On 1 February 1901, the body of Queen Victoria was brought across The Solent and laid in state overnight behind the Guard House of St George Barracks. The following day, many crowned heads of Europe and Scandinavia and their escorts boarded the funeral train, which was drawn up at the Royal Victoria Station. They solemnly accompanied the body to London and thence on to Frogmore and interment.

The funeral was a unique and very important occasion in both the history of the Gosport Railway and the town itself. Many tales could be told about that last royal journey. One will suffice here. The royal train was twenty minutes late because the honourable guests were seated in the wrong positions and had to be reseated!

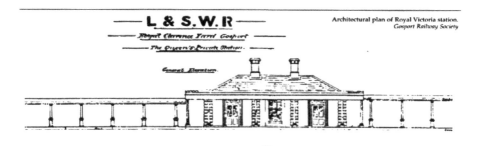

Fragments of the royal station inside the boundaries of Royal Clarence Yard still exist and are a focus for discussions on preservation in or around the marine industrial developments now shaping the south-east corner of Royal Clarence Yard.

WHAT DID GOSPORT STATION LOOK LIKE IN THE EARLY YEARS?

When the line was new, on arrival at the station the average passenger would see a new, semi-classical, 'shining' building, surrounded by a masonry wall, topped with decorative railings. In later years, a hexagonal pillar box of the Pilbeam design was sited just outside the gates.

Gosport's former railway lines have found new use as footpaths, cycle lanes and busways. The 'Triangle' junction in Leesland Park was where the Stokes Bay branch line led off from the main line between Gosport and Fareham. (LM)

The grounds of the station were laid out to lawns and flowerbeds. As passengers walked up along the granite setts, ahead an ornamental garden with shrubs and flowering plants presented itself. Passengers would then walk through the colonnade and, in doing so, pass by the station master's residence at the east end of the building on the right.

GOSPORT STATION DAILY TRADE

The main railway station in Gosport was very busy in the middle of the nineteenth century, particularly with the carriage of coal and other freight. However, the opening of a direct service from London to Portsmouth in 1847 began to have a heavy impact on 'Portsmouth's station in Gosport'. This was how it was known in Portsmouth, but never by that name on the Gosport side of Portsmouth Harbour.

The pay of the railway servants at the time of opening was very little compared with today. In 1842, if a ticket collector worked two hours' overtime on a Sunday, he earned the princely sum of the equivalent of 2p. Even coming forward to the end of that century, a station office lad of 21 only earned 10s a week and a porter's wage was just 15s per week. From this, if the porter was lucky, he could obtain lodgings for around 10s per week, which included bed and meals, his washing done and his clothes mended.

When it came to retirement, the situation was no better. Another member of the extended Belben family, Thomas, worked in the Gosport goods shed. He was a railway servant all his life, and did not retire until after the First World War as he was retained for service. When he did retire, his pension amounted to 16s 9d per week. When he reached the grand old age of 70, he was forced to take the national pension. This was 10s a week and this was deducted from his railway pension. This left him with 6s 9d per week from the railway. So, he divided this small amount between himself and his wife, with he having 3s 9d one week and her 3s, and then the following week, she would have the 3s 9d and he would have the 3s!

From the very sparse service offered by the railway company on the opening of the line, by January 1842 the services had increased to nine return trains a day. For the first sixty years of the history of the line, London trains had to travel via Eastleigh. But in 1903, with the opening of the Meon Valley line, the London trains were directed over this route. It is very strange to think that the Gosport line, although gone now, witnessed both the opening and closing of this country line up through Hampshire to Alton.

An important event to occur at Gosport Station, within four years of its opening, was the installation of the electric telegraph. This resulted from a proposal at a shareholders' meeting. The telegraph line was laid between Gosport and Nine Elms and, at the time of its installation, April 1845, it was the longest stretch of telegraph line in the country.

The telegraph line was available for public use and a charge was made of 3s for a single cable or 5s for a cable with a paid reply. To this service had to be added the cost of delivery of the printed telegram and the length of the message could not exceed forty words.

The telegraph line was keenly used by the Royal Navy to supplement their semaphore towers, which stretched from the Isle of Wight to the Admiralty building in London. The towers were effective in fine weather but bad visibility greatly affected the accuracy of their message sending. The telegraph wire became greatly used, especially when the Portsmouth Signal Tower burnt down at the beginning of the twentieth century.

Towards the end of the passenger service on the Gosport line, an elderly lady told me the following story. It was about 1951 when, after not seeing her cousin for very many years, the two of them decided to meet before it was too late. After a lengthy exchange of letters it was agreed the cousin would come to Gosport and arrive by a certain train and her relative would meet her there. They both worried that after so many years apart they would not recognise each other, so they settled on both wearing a corsage on their coats to make identification easy. The train duly arrived and the Gosport relative excitedly waited on the platform, worrying if they would find each other. They did – neither need have worried as there was only one passenger on that train. No chance of missing each other!

WARTIME AND BEYOND

As the pace of war increased in late 1914, so the role of the station revived as a result of Gosport becoming a major site of victualling to the Royal Navy. Large quantities of all kinds of supplies flowed to and from nearby Royal Clarence Yard.

Large numbers of troop movements took place also. As the First World War progressed, transportation of the wounded to the Royal Naval Hospital Haslar took place.

After the First Word War, rail traffic began to decrease, and in 1934 the twin track to Fareham was singled. In an attempt at economy in 1937, unsuccessful experiments were made with a rubber-tyred, petrol-engined rail bus developed by the French Michelin tyre company.

With the onset of the Second World War, Gosport Station again saw

The rapid-transit Eclipse busway was recently constructed on the former track bed of the main railway line between Gosport and Fareham. (LM)

much military activity, including supply and hospital trains and trains carrying prisoners of war on their way to the internment camps on the Gosport peninsula. On the night of 10 March 1941, the station received a direct incendiary hit in an air attack by the Luftwaffe. The main damage was to the roofing, which caught alight and collapsed.

The end of the hostilities in 1945 once again diminished the Gosport Station role. Long before Dr Beeching wielded his infamous axe to the railways of Britain, the line was threatened with closure. Finally, on 6 June 1953, scheduled passenger services from Gosport ceased. Freight working remained until 30 January 1969, when all rail traffic to Gosport Station ended.

Sections of the platforms and war-damaged buildings were to remain in situ under statutory protection. However, a long period of deterioration and decay to the original station complex set in. Schemes for redevelopment of the site came and went, until relatively recently, when a sensitive and award-winning restoration of the fabric of the original buildings took place to create a residential apartment block (see the contemporary photograph on page 127). Nothing of the goods yard and its ancillary facilities remains visible.

11

PRIDDY'S HARD: REPURPOSING A HISTORIC GUNPOWDER MAGAZINE AND MUNITIONS DEPOT

Giles Pritchard

A SHORT HISTORY OF PRIDDY'S HARD

Priddy's Hard has a long history stretching back over 250 years. The development and expansion of the site to supply the gunpowder and munitions demands of the Royal Navy is a story well worth telling. The site occupies a once-isolated position a mile or two north of Gosport town centre, on the western shore of Portsmouth Harbour, spreading along the northern bank of the tidal inlet known as Forton Lake.

The story really begins in sixteenth-century Portsmouth when the Square Tower (still in situ at the harbour mouth), originally built in 1494 as part of the city's defences, was converted in 1584 to a gunpowder store which served the Royal Naval Dockyard. While this was a suitable building for its purpose in its time, its location at the end of the High Street posed a substantial risk to the local residents. There was always the potential threat of a catastrophic explosion that could destroy the area, should the worst kind of accident happen. A petition to the Master General of Ordnance led in 1764 to a decision to remove the gunpowder from the Square Tower.

In 1750, the Board of Ordnance, via an Act of King George III, purchased 40 acres of agricultural land in Gosport and a boatyard from Jane Priddy and Thomas Missing. An earthen rampart was constructed here to extend the outer western defences of Portsmouth Harbour and the Royal Dockyard.

Former munitions bunkers have been turned into residential units fronting the Forton Lake foreshore at Priddy's Hard. (GP)

Completed in 1757, the land that the rampart enclosed was known as Priddy's Hard Fort and was manned by the army.

On Crown land, the site became one of the possible locations for resiting the gunpowder store from the Square Tower. The other sites were Boatswain's Hill Coppice, Portchester Castle and Horsea Island. Although none of the four locations were considered ideal due to their proximity to the Royal Dockyard, in December 1766 a decision was finally made to relocate the gunpowder stores to Priddy's Hard.

The Board of Ordnance reviewed the preliminary plans of Priddy's Hard in 1769. These provided for a single magazine and a cooperage. The Commanding Royal Engineer at Portsmouth, Captain Archer, was ordered to prepare further plans and estimates. As with many military building projects, Priddy's Hard was designed by committee, with many people contributing to the ideas base for the plan.

Building work on the new powder magazine commenced in 1771, along with the guardhouse, Shifting House barracks, cooperage and an octagonal waterfront harbour loading basin. The Grand Magazine, as it became known, was eventually completed and ready for receiving gunpowder in 1777. The harbour basin, known as the 'Camber', was dredged and ready for boats and a new covered rolling way was completed to connect the magazine to the basin.

During this time, the local residents around the Square Tower continued to petition the board and soon after the completion of the Grand Magazine

The Powder Monkey pub and brewing company is built inside a former gunpowder and artillery shell magazine. (GP)

all the gunpowder barrels were removed from the Square Tower and shipped across to Priddy's Hard.

On the modernisation of the dockyard in the mid-nineteenth century, Priddy's Hard was recommended as the site for new laboratories, where the filling and emptying of cartridges could take place. Previously located at Gunwharf on the Portsmouth shore, the Admiral Superintendent of the Dockyard, Admiral Hyde Parker, considered that the industrialisation of the yard would make the Gunwharf site dangerous.

Plans were drawn up in 1847 for the laboratories and a new 'expense magazine' (army terminology for ready-to-use powder and munitions) to serve them, which would hold 200 barrels. A new landing stage was provided, separate to the camber, which would be left for powder tranship-ment purposes.

The new separate facilities were recognised as the key to safe and efficient working. The new laboratories were completed and all activities relocated there by November 1848. This marked the start of a major transformation of the site from being largely a storage depot to one where explosives were manufactured and manipulated.

In 1860, it was realised that additional space was required for the storage of ammunition and detailed drawings were prepared for a new magazine at Priddy's Hard. A bombproof building was designed and a new rationalised flow system was established, based on a tram system. In 1861, 'C' Magazine

The Grand Magazine, now used for non-warlike purposes such as wedding receptions, is at the centre of this once remote and secretive gunpowder factory and munitions depot of the Royal Navy. (GP)

was completed, a substantial brick building with a barrel-vaulted roof and flanked with earthworks.

Queen's Regulations of 1868 stipulated that no laboratory operations with a risk of explosion could take place within 400 yards of a magazine where large quantities of powder were stored. At Priddy's Hard, 'A' Magazine was less than 100 yards from the laboratories. In 1875, it was decided to build a new magazine and the Magazine Committee recommended that it be located away from the main centre of the established site. So, 1876 saw the construction of a new powder pier to serve this magazine, which was built out from the existing camber.

By 1877, the plans for the new magazine were complete and the building was located in one of the former bastions of the eighteenth-century ramparts. 'E' Magazine, as it was called, was a large single-storey building with two barrel-vaulted chambers and was completed in 1879.

Work on improving the shell-filling facilities and storage continued but the inadequacy of ship berthing arrangements was seen as a major obstacle to progress. Consequently, a new shell pier was commenced in 1879 and the old pier serving the laboratories was abandoned. A new pair of laboratory buildings were designed with an earth traverse between – a shell store and a manipulating room.

In 1883, a shell exploded in the manipulating room, which demolished the building and killed six people. As a result, the decision was made to move this activity outside of the historic fortifications and a new set of shell-filling rooms, a fusing room, an expense magazine and an un-heading room were constructed in 1886–87. These were located along the edge of Forton Creek and were heated by hot-water pipes, supplied from a boiler in the cookhouse. This had been retained when the building was converted from the Small Arms Cartridge Factory.

A complex internal communication system developed, consisting of a 18in-gauge tram road for the powder line and a 30in-gauge line for the shell tramway.

The 1890s saw the introduction of a new explosive called cordite. Its invention resulted in a significant design change for magazine buildings. In 1896–97, new laboratories were constructed for filling cartridges. These consisted of lightweight timber buildings protected by massive earth traverses. They were located adjacent to the eighteenth-century ramparts and the traverses were formed by extending out the banks of the ramparts at right angles. Each building was separated from the next by these traverses, which were capped with concrete to give additional protection from explosion. The ditch of the ramparts was filled in and a wooden tramway constructed.

Following an explosion in the new shell store in 1902, it was decided that the proximity of the site to the naval dockyard was too close for the bulk storage of explosives. Following the opening of a new store in Bedenham, just to the north along the western shore of Portsmouth Harbour, Priddy's Hard became a site for the filling of shells and cartridges and the inspection and repair of rockets, powder cartridges and other munitions.

Significant expansion of Priddy's Hard took place during the First World War, partly because of an increased need for filled cartridges and partly because of the introduction of new explosives such as TNT. The shell-filling rooms of 1886, located along the edge of the ramparts, were converted to TNT shell-filling rooms. Additional buildings were constructed, principally to the west of the ramparts, such as additional mine stores, mine-filling rooms and buildings for new weapons requiring storage, filling and maintenance.

Further buildings were constructed during the Second World War, including air-raid shelters, and some of the existing buildings were adapted. Most of these structures were temporary and very little building took place after 1945.

The laboratories closed in the 1960s, followed by the shell-filling rooms in 1970. The site was finally closed in 1989. Over the past twenty-five years, the site has been partly redeveloped with a new museum, Millennium Promenade, new access bridge across Forton Lake and new housing.

Priddy's Hard has many layers of significance due to its varied history as a Royal Ordnance Yard from the eighteenth to twentieth centuries. As a prominent site located on the edge of the Portsmouth Harbour, it is recognised by national designations including scheduling, listing and protected sites for nature conservation.

The Scheduled Ancient Monument designation covers all of the eighteenth-century earthwork defences at Priddy's Hard, including the earthworks around 'E' Magazine and the area just outside the southern end of the defences. The Grand Magazine, built in 1770–76 and constructed of brickwork with raking buttresses, is grade-I listed.

There are two Grade-II-listed buildings: 'E' Magazine is the largest example of its type and is located within the former demi-bastion of the earlier earthwork defences, and the Quick-Fire Shell Store is the best surviving example of an ordnance yard shell store. Many of the remaining historic buildings are also Grade II listed, including the Camber Basin, the Mines and Countermines Store, 'C' Magazine and the remaining laboratory buildings.

In addition to the statutory listings, the entire Priddy's Hard site lies within the Priddy's Hard Conservation Area, protecting the importance of the site as a Royal Ordnance Yard. The site was designated in 1990.

The rebuilt Hardway Promenade alongside the Portsmouth Harbour foreshore is an airy and scenic approach route into Priddy's Hard from the north side. (GP)

Work in progress. The small harbour of the Camber, directly opposite HM Naval Base Portsmouth, awaits restoration to its former function as the maritime cross-harbour entry and egress point for Priddy's Hard. (GP)

Nature Conservation around the Priddy's Hard site is also of significance, with a number of protected sites. The Convention on Wetlands of International Importance, called the Ramsar Convention, is an intergovernmental treaty that provides the framework for national action and international co-operation for the conservation and wise use of wetlands and their resources. The Ramsar Convention is the only global environmental treaty that deals with a specific ecosystem. The treaty was adopted in the Iranian city of Ramsar in 1971 and the convention's member countries cover all geographic regions of the planet. The coastal edge to all of Priddy's Hard is designated as a Ramsar site.

A Site of Important Nature Conservation (SINC) forms part of a wider national network of non-statutory, locally valued wildlife sites. These are generally administered by local authorities in partnership with conservation organisations. All sites are assessed against detailed criteria developed by HCC, Natural England and the Hampshire & Isle of Wight Wildlife Trust. A site may qualify as a SINC due to the presence of a notable species or an important habitat. In 1998, the ramparts and area north of Forton Lake were designated a SINC.

DEVELOPMENT PROJECT – ENTER PORTSMOUTH NAVAL BASE PROPERTY TRUST (PNBPT)

Since the closure of the naval stores in 1988, Priddy's Hard was vacated by the Royal Navy Artillery Division and GBC took ownership of the site. In 2000, the new millennium footbridge linking the site to Gosport town centre was opened over Forton Lake. This reduced the former isolation of the site, linking Priddy's Hard to the town via the Gosport Waterfront Trail.

The oldest part of the site was opened to the public in 2001 when it was redeveloped as 'Explosion! – The Museum of Naval Firepower'. In 2003, GBC sold on long lease part of the site to residential developer Crest Nicholson, who completed construction of new housing in 2006.

In 2009, the remaining 23-acre site was acquired from GBC by Portsmouth Naval Base Property Trust (PNBPT) with a view to 'developing the site, refurbishing the historic buildings and bringing them into new beneficial use'. Planning permission was granted for new houses within the traverses of the 1886 shell-filling rooms. In 2015, the trust successfully applied for assistance from the Heritage Lottery Fund, as part of the Heritage Enterprise programme, to create new sustainable economic uses for the site and its derelict historic buildings – these were to include residential, commercial and cultural attractions.

REPURPOSING

The development project was part of a long-term strategy for sustainable rejuvenation of landscape features and the built estate, including rescuing features of 'heritage at risk', opening up the museum site, revealing the historic landscape, increasing visitor numbers and providing commercial opportunities to ensure future socioeconomic resilience. The works included the restoration of a number of historically important munitions buildings. Through a combination of conservation works, repairs, access improvements, new interpretation and activities, a new sustainable future for these significant buildings has been achieved.

The wider project also included the creation of new residential properties through the reuse of existing buildings and the construction of new dwellings. This has been led by Elite Homes Ltd, with the capital receipt providing match funding for the Heritage Lottery works.

The brief developed by the trust as part of the Heritage Lottery-funded project has resulted in the implementation of a range of urgently needed

Explosion: The Museum of Naval Firepower is the primary exhibition venue and visitor attraction at Priddy's Hard. (LM)

conservation and access works to the buildings. The project has conserved and enhanced the heritage to bring about a phased improvement to the visitor experience by providing more opportunities for residents and visitors to explore Priddy's Hard.

The brief for the capital works set out the following aims:

- The conservation and reuse of 'E' Magazine to create a new brewery operated by Powder Monkey Brewery, with public access to experience both the brewing process and the interior of the listed building.
- Extensive repairs, including replacement of the collapsed roof to the Proof House, to create a store for the volunteers working on the ramparts and a small interpretation hub where visitors can learn about the site.
- The conservation and conversion of the former Shifting House into a Landmark Trust-style holiday let.
- The conservation and conversion of the former Case Store and Rolling Way into a new Tap House, operated by Powder Monkey Brewery.
- The conservation and alteration of 'C' Magazine to become a base for the volunteers.

- The conservation and alteration of the former Mines and Countermines Store to create a new museum which pays tribute to the high-risk, high-octane operations of the coastal forces in both world wars. Within the exhibition are two Second World War historic boats, (Coastal Motor Boat) CMB331 and (Motor Torpedo Boat) MTB71.
- The conservation and repairs of the former shell store.

At an early stage of the project, a Conservation Statement was prepared for the site to inform all current and future proposals for the care and development of the buildings to minimise harm either to the fabric of the buildings or their architectural character. This included a set of policies that were adopted to act as a basis for decision-making for the future. A full impact assessment and mitigation strategy was prepared and condition surveys undertaken to establish a complete understanding of the context and potential impact of the works.

Throughout the design process, the significance of the heritage assets was carefully considered and informed the design approach. Where internal alterations to the existing buildings were proposed and necessary to deliver the new uses, consideration in each instance was taken to minimise harm to the heritage significance of the buildings while still achieving the aims set out within the brief. All new insertions and alterations were designed to be sympathetic to the historic setting while still being clearly identifiable as modern insertions. The impact of all proposed alterations was assessed within a detailed heritage statement.

Throughout the early stages of the project, extensive consultations were undertaken with GBC and various statutory bodies. The planning officers and the borough conservation officer were supportive of the project ambition and were instrumental in helping drive the project forward. Historic England were also embedded in the decision-making process. However, the needs of the historic buildings had to be balanced against the challenges of flood mitigation and protecting and enhancing the important nature conservation sites. Both Natural England and the Environment Agency were key consultees and a balance had to be reached between all three parties before a definitive planning decision could be determined.

THE POWDER MONKEY BREWERY AND PUB

Converting 'E' Magazine into a new brewery had its own challenges beyond the conversion of the building itself. To enable the magazine to be used as a brewery, the design and layout of the equipment and visitor experience have been carefully considered to limit alteration to the existing fabric.

In order for the equipment to be installed and deliveries stored, an existing window opening was widened on the south elevation to create a new doorway sufficiently wide enough to allow access for a forklift truck. This required the removal of brickwork from the external wall that was up to 3m thick. In addition, two openings were formed in the passageway and traverse supporting walls and a new external working yard created by the removal of parts of the earth banking from around the building. This required a full archaeological survey of the earthwork ramparts and close consultation with Historic England. The original entrances were unblocked to allow staff and visitors to enter via archways formed in the bastion.

Inside the building, design decisions were informed by the building fabric. The structure is divided into two linked chambers – the east side had survived with all is original timbers that formed racking for gunpowder barrels, timber floorboards and overhead gantry crane. The west chamber had suffered from an earlier fire, resulting in the loss of part of the internal structure and floor.

Early consultations with Historic England resulted in an agreement to retain the intact east chamber and to convert it into the public bar area and shop for the brewery, with carefully designed interventions to create a small office, work area and toilet facilities. In the damaged west chamber, it was agreed that the remaining section of floor could be removed to allow a new suspended concrete floor to be installed, to support the brewing vats and to achieve a waterproof surface for washing down. All the removed timbers were reused to repair areas of the floor in the eastern chamber, where they had been extensively damaged by a previous outbreak of dry rot.

The visitor friendly brewing experience gives an opportunity to experience both the building and watch the brewing process first hand. The nearby former case store has been converted to provide a new tap house for the brewery and has become established as a popular destination venue at the heart of Priddy's Hard. Along with enhancing public facilities on the site, the pub is supported by patronage from nearby residents and tourists visiting the various attractions of Priddy's Hard.

The external building fabric has been extensively repaired and the conversion saw the demolition of the southern 1930s extension, which has opened up previously obstructed views of the harbour. The gable end of the existing building has been rebuilt using matching bricks. New glazed folding doors have been fitted to connect the internal and external spaces together.

While design work on the individual buildings around Priddy's Hard progressed, the overall landscape and the spaces between the buildings needed to be fully interpreted for both the existing situation and any future developments. This is of particular importance at Priddy's Hard. Many of the external spaces still have significant features or qualities that are important to the site history, its unique character and sense of place.

While the proposed redevelopment of the site looks to secure a long-term future, in doing so, the PNBPT did not want to lose the qualities that make Priddy's Hard unique. A detailed study was undertaken to fully understand and record the existing landscape, which could be used to define a set of clear principles to determine any future development.

There was, for example, evidence of the use of black ash, clinker and coal as external surfacing materials. It is believed these were used because of their incombustible nature – crucial in any factory involved in gunpowder manipulation! Today on site, there are some remnants of previous external surfaces and demolished buildings. These include areas of concrete, asphalt and some of the rails from the once-extensive tramway system. However, much of the original surfacing has been lost or is below new surfaces.

The development of Priddy's Hard has created complex layers and mosaics of buildings and landscapes that have built up over time. Much of the north-east of the site, while seeing a large amount of intervention, remained as grassed areas. Most of the south-eastern sections were developed, creating a much denser industrial landscape and many of the spaces between buildings would have had hard surfaces of asphalt, concrete, black ash and paving (pitched and flags).

There is evidence of trees and grassed plots. In particular, the 'green' in front of the main office block, which has been there since the middle of the nineteenth century. It became important that this unique language of historic surfaces be used to inform the choice of surfacing when developing the site for future uses. While additional landscaping proposals are yet to be fully decided upon, it was established that the historic surfaces that remain should be retained and built into the new external landscape.

Clearance of vegetation from the ramparts scheduled monument has been undertaken to protect and reveal the historic earthworks. This is designed to improve public access to and understanding of the site, facilitate adjacent development works and improve the aesthetic value of the site. Indeed, the ramparts may become a public park in the not-too-distant future. Gorse, dense scrub, self-seeded small trees and tall ruderal plant species that colonised the earthworks have been removed. Views have been opened up. Some scattered trees and native vegetation have, however, been retained across the site.

THE VISION

The project to convert the first seven historic buildings and the development of new housing on the vacant parts of the site is the first phase of works to be completed by the PNBPT. However, the story does not end there. The PNBPT vision and determination to bring this challenging site back into public and cultural use, along with the supporting stakeholders (GBC, Historic England, the Heritage Lottery Fund and other major funders), was possibly the last chance for the remaining buildings at Priddy's Hard to be saved from demolition and for its long and fascinating story to be kept broadly intact for future generations to come. The ambition of the trust is to complete the successful repurposing of this site in the coming years, repairing and adapting the remaining buildings, providing new developments as considered appropriate and completing the restoration and improvements to the landscape setting.

Note
Giles Pritchard is a specialist conservation architect and director of the company Pritchard Architecture, who were the lead architects on the Priddy's Hard Development Project.

12

THE HOVERCRAFT MUSEUM:
POTENTIAL AND ISSUES
AT SOLENT AIRPORT,
LEE-ON-THE-SOLENT

Brian Mansbridge

Seaplane Square got its name during the First World War when the site was temporarily requisitioned to train naval seaplane pilots for anti-submarine patrols. Then, in 1918, the seafront site became a permanent seaplane base and some of its unique characteristics remain. Much later, the slipway and hangars proved ideal to support hovercraft operations that developed out of the magnificent invention of the hovercraft by Sir Christopher Cockerell (1910–99).

THE HOVERCRAFT CONNECTION

In 1962, the slipway and the square were brought back into use by visits from the early hovercraft built in the Solent area, leading to the formation of the Interservice Hovercraft Trials Unit. This was set up to evaluate the capability of this unique British invention in military roles. It also worked with government and industry to improve the early models and their capabilities. Subsequently, in January 1976, the joint service unit was renamed the Naval Hovercraft Trials Unit, primarily to explore the naval role in mine clearance, due to the relative invulnerability of hovercraft to sea mines.

In the mid 1980s, in an attempt to save the last of the Hovertravel SRN5 Warden-Class craft, local enthusiasts and the Hovercraft Society managed to store the remaining SRN5 and other early generation craft in various garages and barns in the Solent area. Warwick Jacobs, a founding member of the museum, was successful in persuading Captain David Newbery RN, who was winding down HMS *Daedalus*, to store the rescued BH7, a military trials hovercraft, at the former hovercraft base.

At about the same time, the newly formed Hovercraft Museum Trust, a registered charity, arranged a lease on the site and was able to utilise the hangars to consolidate craft storage within the former hovercraft base, not just collecting all types of this unique British invention, but for restoration works and eventually arrangements to open the site to the public as a museum. This leasing arrangement continued even after the military left the site in 1996 and site control passed to a government land agent.

The collection of early experimental and military hovercraft increased. In addition, amateur enthusiasts donated all sorts of idiosyncratic craft and racing hovercraft. The variety of craft and exhibitions grew significantly and the public were fascinated with this new form of transport being exhibited. Annual 'Hovershows', with hovercraft trips, attracted as many as 5,000 visitors.

SRN5, an early craft at the Interservice Hovercraft Trails Unit, is now on the Historic Ships Register. The author of this chapter piloted this craft during training in 1975. (BP)

A bird's eye view of the Hovercraft Museum site at Lee-on-the-Solent. (HM)

WAS THERE A FUTURE FOR THIS FORM OF TRANSPORT?

While the public fascination with hovercraft remained strong, it gradually became clear, even to the most ardent manufacturers and operators, that this novel form of transport could not compete commercially with much cheaper to operate displacement vessels for fare-paying trips. The exception being in short, high-volume ferry journeys like the still active ten-minute Solent crossing from Southsea beach to Ryde, on the Isle of Wight.

This is because the hovercraft has to lift its load on air generated by a fan, as well as move the craft forward with a propellor. This is somewhat akin to a helicopter, although that uses the same rotor to lift and move. The hovercraft, in addition to the fuel cost, requires the maintenance of the rubber skirt. This essential task is costly and demanding in manpower hours to repair. Skirt maintenance is not such a regular problem in sheltered waters like The Solent, where operating speeds are usually less than 40 knots. But in open waters like the English Channel, with larger craft and operating speeds of 60 knots, it could become a nightly task, especially during periods of heavy weather. Similarly, for distance travel, the hovercraft cannot compete with the fixed-wing aeroplane that generates 'free lift' by the design of the wings as it moves. Or with the more versatile helicopter, which has similar high maintenance and fuel costs, but not the same rubber skirt to maintain.

Nonetheless, the hovercraft does have some unique advantages in its ability to carry heavy loads over difficult surfaces like ice, marshland and shallows. The military recognised that it offered distinct advantages in an amphibious assault role. It could take tanks and troops from sea, over mines, beach defences and even penetrate to safe areas inland, and all at high speed.

Manufacturers have been able to improve on the original aircraft designs, which were somewhat over-engineered and not best suited to saltwater environments, utilising well-matched engineering. Today, a smaller number of specialist manufacturers still build hovercraft, with designs to maximise the amphibious benefits while reducing operating costs.

Changes that left us many experimental hovercraft, as witness to the evolution of the invention, together with manufacturers' blueprints, drawings, trials records, etc., form an archive of documentation of national and international significance. All this original material is a legacy – in the historic context, one that is irreplaceable. This comprehensive collection, co-located to The Solent, where the invention was first demonstrated and developed, has more than filled the museum!

In 2000, the Hovercraft Museum moved into the big league as it acquired machines of the SRN4 Mountbatten Class. For over thirty years, these craft were engaged in cross-Channel services and were being stretched and improved until the huge Mk3 craft could take sixty-two cars and 423 passengers across the busy waters of the Dover Straits. They still hold

The last of its kind. The giant car-carrying SRN4 hovercraft Princess Anne *deployed for decades, from the early 1970s, on the cross-Channel service between Dover and Boulogne. (BP)*

the record for the fastest seagoing English Channel crossing from Dover to Calais and Boulogne. In June 2019, HRH Princess Anne honoured the museum with a visit commemorating the 50th anniversary of her launching the craft. She toured the museum, met with volunteers and unveiled a plaque commemorating her visit.

In 2016, Homes England, the current museum site agent, obtained ownership of the SRN4s from the entrepreneur who bought them after their cross-Channel service ended. The site agent was expecting to scrap the craft to clear the site for sale. This despite the fact that these large craft were the museum's principal public attraction. In two days, more than 10,000 people signed a museum initiative petitioning to retain an SRN4 as part of Britain's unique hovercraft heritage. A deal was reached with Homes England to retain the *Princess Anne* on a short-term lease. The other SRN4, *Princess Margaret*, was scrapped, releasing Seaplane Square to be re-let by the land agent as an (ongoing) lorry park for large articulated trucks.

THE HOVERCRAFT MUSEUM TODAY

The museum is run entirely by volunteers. It contains the world's largest library on hovercraft history: in excess of 18,000 books, publications, films, videos, models, photographs and drawings. The main hangars contain exhibitions about hovercraft development. Within the hangars and around them is a range of hovercraft exhibits from experimental craft to variants of the first commercial and military models, as well as a large collection of smaller craft. Despite the irreplaceable nature of this collection, due to the insecurity of tenure, the museum is not able to apply for heritage funding or provide better safekeeping for its exhibits and artifacts.

The museum survives – just – on day-to-day income from gate receipts and the generosity of enthusiasts and supporters. All administration, visitor services, restoration and maintenance works are undertaken by unpaid volunteers. Prior to the Covid pandemic, the museum had to close for a period while unsafe buildings were repaired. Then, just as it was recovering from this downturn, the Covid 19 lockdown curtailed all gate receipts. Fortunately, the trustees obtained an extraordinary 'Covid 19 gap grant', which paid the site rent during lockdown and in July 2021 it was able to open to visitors following Covid-safe guidelines.

One for the future. The currently empty but still impressive and listed Wardroom Block on the Daedalus *site is adjacent to the Hovercraft Museum. Its repurposed future is yet to be … repurposed! (LM)*

WHAT ABOUT THE FUTURE FOR THE MUSEUM?

The future of the museum is far from secure. The site is still former MoD land and currently on market-negotiable status with new agencies such as the Daedalus Development Corporation as part of the waterfront brownfield development area. Its earlier sale was only stalled by the complications that arose from the site's military legacy and the listed buildings. Historic England, together with GBC, is working within the recently formulated Gosport HAZ scheme, helping to identify the development potential of the site, particularly the reuse of the listed buildings.

No doubt most developers would like to turn the attractive seafront views into profitable high-rise flats. Finding the right developer who is able to develop the whole site, balancing the needs with a mix of industry, housing and the sensitive reuse of the listed buildings, is a more challenging task. It needs a developer with a repurposed vision for the whole site. Hopefully, that does include acting as a saviour for the Hovercraft Museum and its collection of hovercraft and related archives. Given appropriate support, the Hovercraft Museum could complement the nearby and now highly visible Portsmouth and Gosport Museums as a transportation hub, with hovercraft

A manufacturing success story. The transition at Solent Airport from active naval aviation to civilian flying is mirrored in the success of the Britten-Norman Aviation Company, which assembles the widely exported twin-engine Islander from Hangars West on the airfield. (LM)

The new modular units of the Daedalus Park Industrial Estate are indicative of modern commercial imperatives for former brownfield sites such as Solent Airport. (LM)

combining with local air, railway and transport collections, few of which currently enjoy permanent or ideal exhibition venues. A combined museum complex formed around Seaplane Square, with shared services and facilities and based on a central heritage transport theme, would constitute a visitor attraction and not just for the Gosport and Fareham area but for the United Kingdom as a whole. And what an attraction it would be if it was linked to the nearby Portsmouth Historic Dockyard sites by hovercraft …

In real economic terms, the land costs in this prime seafront location are beyond local borough council financial resources. However, in terms of heritage value to the nation, a world-unique Hovercraft Museum is worthy of a place in the pantheon of British manufacturing industry history. Local interest in the listed buildings that are part of the site's original seaplane ancestry and the craft on the Historic Ships Register can and should grow into something more.

The museum site and its collections should be considered a national asset – one that is quite irreplaceable. Let us hope that this extraordinarily unique example of British manufacturing heritage is not lost to future generations. Sir Christopher Cockerell needs us all to safeguard the collection of all that his genius gave to the world!

NOTES ON THE CONTRIBUTORS

KEVIN CASEY

Kevin is the vice chair of the Historical Diving Society and director of their Diving Museum. He is keenly interested in heritage and history, especially relating to Gosport and diving, having worked as a commercial diver for forty years around the world. Since 2015, he has worked on fundraising to restore No. 2 Battery and develop the Diving Museum. Kevin has served on The Gosport Society committee for almost ten years and the Friends of Stokes Bay committee for thirty.

SUE COURTNEY

Sue Courtney is a primary school teacher, an executive style coach and a reiki tutor. She has a keen interest in history, being vice chairman of The Gosport Society 2018–22 and a representative on the Gosport HODs committee. She has written articles for the *Surrey Times*, *Gosport and Fareham Sunday Globe* Online, the *Sol Times* in Spain and other publications in print and kindle form, available on Amazon.

ROBERT HARPER

Robert is a long-serving heritage, conservation and design officer at GBC. His professional duties place him at the centre of development planning in the Borough of Gosport. This includes reviews and analysis of proposals for development in existing conservation areas; advocacy for listing buildings; commentary on proposed extensions to or creating of new conservation areas, such as Stokes Bay and considerations of design briefs for the built estate in Gosport. He is also an important committee representative to the HAZ Partnership, standing committees at GBC, and liaison with Historic England and external agencies.

PETER KEAT

Peter is a long-standing and principal figure in Gosport Railway Society (GRS). He has written numerous books and articles on the (former) network of railways on the Gosport peninsula. Much of his work is informed via the tradition of oral history – verbatim accounts provided by former railwaymen, passengers, ancillary workers and residents in and around Gosport and Fareham. The GRS has amassed a comprehensive collection of photographic images of Gosport railways, indicative documentation and line drawings of railway structures dating from the Victorian period.

BRIAN MANSBRIDGE

Brian Mansbridge served in the Royal Navy and trained in mine warfare, diving and as a hovercraft pilot, and was awarded the MBE in the Gulf War. A varied career saw him living in Hong Kong, the USA and Dubai. After naval service, he served the NHS as a Non-Executive Director. His interests include inland waterways, which he toured in his own narrowboat.

Brian retired with his wife to Lee-on-the-Solent and is active on the planning committee of the Lee Residents Association. He assists at the Hovercraft Museum and the parish church of St Faith's.

Brian has two adult children, one running an international school at Haarlem in the Netherlands, and the other working for the Foreign Office.

RICHARD MARTIN

A lifelong Gosportian, Richard Martin was educated at Gosport County Grammar School, during which time he developed a keen interest in the history and topography of his home town. This widened to a passion for English watercolours and ultimately, in 1980, to the founding of the Richard Martin Gallery in Stoke Road in Gosport.

LOUIS MURRAY

Louis Murray is a former university lecturer in the social sciences in universities in England and Australia and chairman of The Gosport Society 2017–22. He is a widely published writer on geographical topics and of walking guides with a heritage, landscape and conservation focus. Louis is also an active member of the Ramblers Association and a life member of the Solent Steam Packet Ltd. He is married with one adult son, an astrophysicist who is resident in Bristol.

MALCOLM STEVENS (1947-2022)

Born, brought up in, and a lifelong resident of Gosport, Malcolm Stevens was a former architect and local government strategic housing manager. His association with Bury House, which is the location of the administrative centre of the Gosport Community Association (GCA), dated from 1973. He was secretary of the GCA from 1979 to 1985. He then became secretary of the Royal Marine Light Infantry Cadet Marching Band for 26 years until the unit was disbanded. Malcolm retired in 2013. In retirement he continued with an interest in local history and genealogy. Malcolm offered his services to GCA to research the long history of Bury House and its residents spanning more than 300 years. This work formed part of the GCA heritage Project. This led in turn to membership of The Gosport Society and becoming Honorary Secretary in 2018, a position Malcolm held with distinction until his death aged 75 on 4th October 2022.

GILES PRITCHARD

Giles Pritchard is an award-winning specialist conservation architect and director of Pritchard Architecture (since 2017). The company operates from offices in the historic Royal Dockyard/ HM Naval Base in Portsmouth. He worked for eighteen years for HCC Architects and is the retained architect of PNBPT and consultant adviser to Historic England and the Diocese of Oxford.

MARGARET VENTHAM

Along with teaching at a nearby secondary school, Margaret's interest in offshore sailing brought her to Gosport. She became a member of the Friends of Gosport Museum in 2006. At a subsequent AGM, she answered the request for museum assistance to become a volunteer. Her first task was to audit the Reserve Map Collection. This required a year of weekly visits to the museum, each lasting three and a half hours. This work transformed Margaret's knowledge of Gosport. Other audits followed, including a favourite one of estate agents, the Grove Estate and papers (undonated) from the ancient church of St Mary the Virgin at Rowner. These were subsequently consigned to the Hampshire Records Office. Margaret continues her voluntary work, currently occupying the chair of the Friends of Gosport Museum committee.

ROBERT WHITELEY

Robert spent most of his adult life involved with education, partially in teaching and eighteen years in local education administration in Stockport, Cheshire. When he retired in 1997, he moved to Gosport and joined both The Gosport Society and the Friends of Gosport Museum. Robert served as secretary of the latter for a few years, then as its president. For the past twenty-five years, he has been able to enjoy his lifelong interest in history and ancient buildings, as well as living in part of Grange Farmhouse, which is thought to be the oldest continually inhabited residential building in Gosport.

SELECT BIBLIOGRAPHY

This list should be considered an entry point for municipal planners, conservation and heritage specialists, local historians and scholars who are interested in researching further the history and heritage of the 800-year-old Borough of Gosport. Most of what may be called the classic statements on Gosport are included below. These are available in book form on open shelves in the libraries of HCC and, importantly, in the local studies collection of the Gosport Discovery Centre (public library) in the High Street in Gosport.

In addition, GBC indicative planning reports as listed on heritage and conservation policies may be accessed through the council website.

The fifty-year publication record of The Gosport Society can be found in the society half-centenary publication listed below. The society publication list now forms a vitally important print archive of much of the socioeconomic development that has occurred in Gosport since 1970, as well as more academically formal histories of people and places.

Like many towns with a long and colourful history, Gosport has a number of keen local historians and enthusiasts, who are outside a formal affiliation to history and voluntary societies. Their work is often individualistic, self-published and sometimes iconoclastic. This literature rarely makes it to commercial shelves for retail sale. Nevertheless, it is an important part of the database and the narrative on Gosport. Examples of this genre are included in the print reference list.

Aylott, R., *Gosport: Two Views. A Photographic Record of the Town from the 1880s to the 1980s* (Alverstoke: Front Page Books, 1983).

Birbeck, E., and A. Ryder, *The Royal Hospital Haslar: A Pictorial History* (Chichester: Phillimore, 2010).

Brown, R., *Are You Being Served? A Reminder of Some of the Shops and Businesses that Flourished in the Gosport of Yesteryear* (Horndean: Southern Press and Milestone Publications, 1982).

Brown, R., *The Story of Lee-on-the-Solent: A Nostalgic Reminder of a Victorian Dream* (Horndean: Milestone Publications, 1982).

Brown, R., *Gosport's Pictorial Past* (Horndean: Milestone Publications, 1983).

Bull, J., *The Night they Blitzed the Ritz: Memoirs of a Bomb Alley Kid* (St John, Jersey: Channel Island Publishing, 2008).

Budden, D.R.P., *Ann's Hill Cemetery: Notes on the War Graves* (Gosport: The Discovery Centre, 1997).

Burton, L., *The Life and Times of Gosport County Grammar School 1902–1972* (Gosport: Burton Publishing, 1989).

Burton, L., and B. Musselwhite, *The Story of Gosport* (Revised edition of the original by Leonard White. Southampton: Ensign Publications, 1989).

Burton, L., and B. Musselwhite, *The Book of Gosport: Celebrating a Distinctive Coastal Town* (Tiverton: Halsgrove, 2004).

Burton, L., and B. Peacey, *Lee-on-the-Solent* (Stroud: The History Press, 2008).

Clark, C., and M. Marks, *Barracks, Forts and Ramparts: 2020 Regeneration Challenges for Portsmouth Harbour's Defence Heritage* (Portsmouth: Tricorn Books, 2020).

Crown Estates, *Gosport: St George Barracks South* (London: Crown Estates with Gosport Borough Council, 1999).

Donald Insall Associates, 'Stokes Bay, Gosport: Designation Assessment Report, Second Draft' (Oxford: Insall-Architects, 2021).

Edelman, I., *Gosport: The Archive Photograph Series* (Stroud: Chalford Publishing, 1995).

Edelman, I., *Gosport: A Pictorial History* (Chichester: Phillimore, 1993).

Gifford Partners, 'Earthwork Survey: The Western Ramparts, Royal Clarence Yard, Gosport', Report B1790, R22, Rev A. (1999).

Gosport Borough Council, 'Gosport Borough Local Plan 2011–29' (adopted 2015).

Gosport Borough Council, 'Draft Stokes Bay Policy Plan' (1981).

Gosport Borough Council, 'Retail Study for Gosport' (London: Hillier Parker with GBC, 1998).

Gosport Borough Council, 'Priddy's Hard Heritage Area: Development Framework' (1999).

Gosport Heritage Open Days, *Remembering the Unforgettable – Four Long years – Peace at Last: A Resource Guide to Gosport and its People during the Great War* (Gosport: HODS, 2018).

Gosport Society, 'Gosport Waterfront and Town Centre SPD Draft Consultation Report – Gosport Society Response' (2017).

Gosport Society, *Gosport 2020 – For the Record: Essays in Celebration of the Half-Centenary of The Gosport Society* (2020).

Hamblin, A., *Alverstoke: The Sequel to 'If Only These Walls Could Speak'* (Kings Langley: Alpine Press, 2011).

Hampshire Preservation Buildings Trust (HPBT) Ltd, *Building Conservation in Hampshire and the Isle of Wight* Chandlers Ford: HPBT, 2019).

Hewitt, P., *Gosport Then and Now: Postcards from Gosport* (Derby: Breedon Books, 2009).

Historic England, *Gosport Heritage Action Zone Delivery Plan* (London/Swindon: Historic England with Gosport Borough Council, 2019).

Hollands, D., *Hampshire's Military Heritage* (Stroud: Amberley Publishing, 2018).

Keat, P.J., *Rails to the Tower: The Lee-on-the-Solent Railway* (Gosport: Gosport Railway Society, Third Impression, 1995).

Keat, P.J., *Goodbye to Victoria, the Last Queen Empress: The Story of Queen Victoria's Funeral Train* (Usk, Monmouth: The Oakwood Press, 2001).

Lee Residents Association, *A History of HMS Daedalus: RNAS Lee-on-the-Solent* (Lee-on-the-Solent: Lee Residents Association with Paul Francis and the Airfield Research Group, undated).

Marden, D., *The Hidden Railways of Portsmouth and Gosport* (Southampton: Kestrel Railway Books, 2011).

Miller, P., *Provincial: The Gosport and Fareham (Buses) Story* (Glossop: Transport Publication Company, 1981).

Mitchell, V., and K. Smith, *Branch Lines Around Gosport* (Midhurst: Middleton Press, 1986).

Moore, D., 'Fort Brockhurst and the Gomer and Elson Forts', *Solent Papers* No. 6 (Gosport: David Moore Publications, 1990).

Moore, D., 'Fort Gilkicker', *Solent Papers* No. 5 (second edition, Gosport: David Moore Publications, 1990).

Murray, L., 'A Walk around the Alver Valley Country Park', *Hampshire Rambler*, July 2011, pp. 4–5 (2011).

Murray, L., 'In Search of Richard Foster Carter (1810–1876): Fragments of the Life of a Victorian Clergyman', *The Hampshire Family Historian* 38(3), pp. 174–76 (2011).

Murray, L., 'Emily Hester Brodrick (1846–1906): A Life Lived in Two Dimensions', *The Hampshire Family Historian* 43(3), pp. 136–37 (2016).

Murray, L., *The Gosport Society 1970–2020: The First Fifty Years* (Lee-on-the-Solent: The Gosport Society in association with LDJ Educational 2020).

Murray, L., *20 Historic Walks in and around Gosport and Fareham* (LDJ Educational in association with The Gosport Society, 2021).

Portsmouth/Gosport/Fareham Teachers Resource Centres, 'The Gosport Lines – Number 1 Bastion Trail' (1982).

Petch, M., *Gosport and Horndean Tramways* (Midhurst: Middleton Press, 1997).

Pre-Construct Archaeology Ltd, *Archaeological Excavation: Phases D1, D2 and D3, Royal Clarence Yard, Gosport* (London, Brockley Business Centre: PCAL, 2009).

Roberts, M., *The Margaret Roberts Local History Collection: Books 1, 2 and 3* (Gosport: The Discovery Centre with Hampshire County Council, publication undated).

Robertson, K., *The Railways of Gosport* (Kevin Robertson and Kingfisher Productions, 1986).

Sadden, J., *Keep the Home Fires Burning: The Story of Portsmouth and Gosport in World War 1* (Portsmouth Publishing and Printing Ltd, 1990).

St Mary's Church, Alverstoke, *An Alverstoke Alphabet* (St Mary's Church, 2012).

Thinking Place, *The Gosport Story* (Thinking Place with GBC, 2021).

Whiteley, R., *Stepping Stones of Time (1290–2000) at Grange Farm, Rowner* (Gosport: The Friends of Gosport Museum, 2000).

INTERNET AND WEBSITE SOURCES OF INFORMATION

Like most places in this internet and digital information era, Gosport is liberally provided with, and informed by, numerous voluntary organisation websites, social media platforms and internet-based repositories of information. Some are stable over time, others wax and wane according to the interests and motives of the site proprietor. An annotated selection is provided here.

Voluntary Organisations with an Interest in Heritage and Conservation

en-gb.facebook.com/angleseyconservationgroup
www.daedalusaviation.org/gosport.aviation.society
fogm.org.uk/joinfriends-gosport-museum
www.friendsofstokesbay.co.uk
gosportrailwaysociety.blogspot.com
www.gosportsociety.co.uk

Museums and Galleries

www.divingmuseum.co.uk
www.hampshire.org.uk/gosport-gallery
www.hovercraft-museum.org
www.nmrn.org.uk/our-museum/explosion
www.nmrn.org.uk/our-museum/submarine
www.richardmartingallery.co.uk

www.yellowedgegallery.com

GENERAL INFORMATION AND TOPIC-SPECIFIC ONLINE SOURCES

www.discovergosport.co.uk – This site generally treats Gosport as a visitor or tourist destination, listing attractions, events and things to do.

www.gosport.info/gosport-people – The site relates stories of mostly historical figures who feature prominently down the ages in the story of Gosport. The site is also a repository for the memories of Gosport residents and nostalgic accounts of yesteryear in the town and surrounds.

www.gosporttowncentre.co.uk – Essentially a commercial and business index, exploring the retail and commercial properties of the High Street and nearby business parks.

www.gva.org.uk – The Gosport Voluntary Action site, which describes its main functions as offering a range of care and community support services to the people of Gosport. This includes para-NHS support networks.

www.thorngatehalls.co.uk – Based in Bury House on Bury Road, the Gosport Community Association (GCA) uses its site as a clearing-house for publicising the wide range of social, cultural and recreational opportunities that occur in and around the multipurpose Thorngate Halls throughout the year.

www.gosportheritage.co.uk – A go-to site for Heritage Open Days listings every September, and for general information on the heritage estate of Gosport.

www.mygosport.org – An around-the-town-wards website covering visual and graphic information on Alverstoke, Bridgemary, Elson, Forton, Rowner, Crofton, Peel Common and Lee-on-the-Solent.

www.developing.gosport.gov.uk – A local-authority-sponsored site that explains the economic opportunities in the borough and business incentive schemes that can be tapped into for companies planning to relocate to Gosport.

www.localhistories.org/gosport/html – For anyone wanting to know, in synoptic terms, the history of Gosport. Probably a first point-of-reference site for historians and research scholars.

www.leeresidentsassociation.co.uk – This dedicated site for residents of Lee-on-the-Solent is politically astute, very well informed about municipal development plans in and for this 'township', within the wider Borough of Gosport, and carries a comprehensive listing of social and cultural activities in its area of interest.

www.gosport.gov.uk – This is the website of the municipality: the Borough of Gosport. Its many divisions explain the responsibilities under law of the GBC to council-tax paying residents and the wider community. For matters to do with housing, rental payments, council tax, planning applications, endorsed conservation areas, environmental and waste management, public recreation and leisure facilities or business opportunities, this is the site to make use of.

www.visit-hampshire.co.uk – This site describes the locations and services provided by Tourist Information Centres across the county. Primarily, this is a HCC and Tourism South-East initiative and listing. It includes the dedicated Tourist Information Centre located adjacent to the Gosport ferry/bus station complex at the harbour end of the High Street in Gosport. That particular office, which also sells a range of gifts and books about Gosport, is also the booking agency for HODs events and similar public exhibitions and activities. A counter service with public access means that real-time advice and information about Gosport can be given to the casual visitor.

Facebook

Recent estimates suggest around 20,000 people, approximately a quarter of the borough population, access and make use of GosportAware, the main Facebook page for the town and its people. To participate in the lively and often friendly exchanges and discussions, you first need to set up a conventional Facebook account with a link to GosportAware. The Gosport Tourist Information Centre also maintains an active Facebook link.

INDEX

Note: *italicised* page references denote illustrations